First World War
and Army of Occupation
War Diary
France, Belgium and Germany

16 DIVISION
Divisional Troops
157 Field Company Royal Engineers
19 December 1915 - 31 March 1919

WO95/1965/3

The Naval & Military Press Ltd
www.nmarchive.com
Published in association with The National Archives

Published by

The Naval & Military Press Ltd

Unit 10 Ridgewood Industrial Park,

Uckfield, East Sussex,

TN22 5QE England

Tel: +44 (0) 1825 749494

www.naval-military-press.com

www.nmarchive.com

This diary has been reprinted in facsimile from the original. Any imperfections are inevitably reproduced and the quality may fall short of modern type and cartographic standards.

© **Crown Copyright**
Images reproduced by permission of The National Archives, London, England, 2015.

Contents

Document type	Place/Title	Date From	Date To
Heading	WO95/1965. 16 Division Headquarters Branches & Services Dec 1915-March 1919 157 Field Company Royal Engineers		
Heading	16th Division 157th Field Coy R.E. Dec 1915-Mar 1919		
Heading	157 Fd. Co. R.E Dec. Vol 1		
War Diary	Blackdown	19/12/1915	19/12/1915
War Diary	Farnborough	19/12/1915	19/12/1915
War Diary	Southampton	19/12/1915	19/12/1915
War Diary	Havre	20/12/1915	21/12/1915
War Diary	Choques	22/12/1915	22/12/1915
War Diary	Mazingarbe	22/12/1915	31/12/1915
Heading	157th F.C.R.E. Vol 2 Jan		
War Diary	Mazingarbe	01/01/1916	31/01/1916
Heading	157th F.C.R.E. Vol. 3		
War Diary	Mazingarbe	01/02/1916	14/02/1916
War Diary	Amettes	14/02/1916	29/02/1916
War Diary	La. Miquellerie	29/02/1916	29/02/1916
Heading	157 F C R E Vol 4		
War Diary	La Miquellerie	01/03/1916	05/03/1916
War Diary	Annequin	05/03/1916	16/03/1916
War Diary	Cauchy-A-La Tour	16/03/1916	27/03/1916
War Diary	Philosophe	27/03/1916	30/06/1916
Miscellaneous			
Heading	War Diary 157th Field Coy Royal Engrs 1st. July to 31st. July 1916. Volume No. 8		
War Diary	Philosophe	01/07/1916	31/07/1916
Heading	War Diary 157th Field Coy R.E Month Of August, 1916. Volume 9		
War Diary	Philosophe	01/08/1916	24/08/1916
War Diary	Ruitz	24/08/1916	25/08/1916
War Diary	Marles Les Mines	25/08/1916	29/08/1916
War Diary	Longeau	30/08/1916	30/08/1916
War Diary	Sailly Le Sec	30/08/1916	31/08/1916
War Diary	Happy Valley Camp	31/08/1916	31/08/1916
Heading	War Diary 157th Field Company R.E For Month Of September 1916. Volume 10		
War Diary	Happy Valley	01/09/1916	03/09/1916
War Diary	Citadel	03/09/1916	06/09/1916
War Diary	Briqueterie	06/09/1916	07/09/1916
War Diary	Guillemont	07/09/1916	10/09/1916
War Diary	Minden Post	10/09/1916	10/09/1916
War Diary	Morlancourt	10/09/1916	11/09/1916
War Diary	Morlancourt	11/09/1916	11/09/1916
War Diary	Sailly Le Sec	11/09/1916	17/09/1916
War Diary	La Chaussee	18/09/1916	18/09/1916
War Diary	Sailly Le Sec	18/09/1916	18/09/1916
War Diary	La Neuville	18/09/1916	18/09/1916
War Diary	Erondelle	18/09/1916	21/09/1916
War Diary	Pont Remy	21/09/1916	21/09/1916

War Diary	Bailleul	21/09/1916	22/09/1916
War Diary	Kemmel	22/09/1916	30/09/1916
Heading	War Diary Month Of October, 1916. Volume II 157th Field Co. RE		
War Diary	Kemmel	01/10/1916	31/10/1916
Heading	War Diary For Month Of November, 1916. Volume 12 157th Field Coy. R.E		
War Diary	Kemmel	01/11/1916	30/11/1916
Heading	War Diary For Month Of December, 1916. Volume 13. 157th Field Coy. RE		
War Diary	Kemmel	01/12/1916	31/12/1916
Heading	War Diary for month of January, 1917. Volume 14. Royal Engineers 157th Field Compy Vol 14		
War Diary	Kemmel	01/01/1917	31/01/1917
Heading	War Diary For Month Of February, 1917. Volume 15 Unit. 157th Field Coy RE		
War Diary	Kemmel	01/02/1917	28/02/1917
Heading	War Diary For Month Of March, 1917 Volume 16 Unit. 157th Field Company RE		
War Diary	Kemmel	01/03/1917	31/03/1917
Heading	War Diary For Month Of April, 1917. Volume. 17 Unit. 157th Field Coy RE		
War Diary	Kemmel	01/04/1917	20/04/1917
War Diary	Mont Rouge	21/04/1917	30/04/1917
Heading	War Diary Volume. 18 For Month Of May, 1917. Unit. 157th Fd Coy Royal Engineers		
War Diary	Mont Rouge	01/05/1917	11/05/1917
War Diary	Chatham Camp (Locre)	12/05/1917	16/05/1917
War Diary	Chatham Camp	17/05/1917	31/05/1917
Heading	War Diary. For Month Of June, 1917. Volume 19 Unit. 157th Field Company RE		
War Diary	Chatham Camp	01/06/1917	07/06/1917
War Diary	Beaver Farm	08/06/1917	09/06/1917
War Diary	Chatham Camp	10/06/1917	13/06/1917
War Diary	York Rd	14/06/1917	18/06/1917
War Diary	Merris	19/06/1917	20/06/1917
War Diary	Eecke	21/06/1917	21/06/1917
War Diary	Poperinghe	22/06/1917	30/06/1917
Operation(al) Order(s)	157th Field Company R.E. Operation Order No. 1	03/06/1917	03/06/1917
Heading	War Diary. For Month Of July, 1917. Volume. 20 Unit 157th Field Coy RE		
War Diary	Poperinghe	01/07/1917	15/07/1917
War Diary	Winnizeele	16/07/1917	26/07/1917
War Diary	Watou	27/07/1917	31/07/1917
Heading	War Diary. For Month Of August, 1917. Volume 21 Unit 157th Field Company RE		
War Diary		01/08/1917	22/08/1917
War Diary	Achiet-Le-Petit	23/08/1917	29/08/1917
War Diary	Hamelincourt	31/08/1917	31/08/1917
Miscellaneous	Operation Orders By O.C. 157th. (Field) Coy. R.E.	15/08/1917	15/08/1917
Miscellaneous	Table Of Work		
Heading	War Diary. For Month Of September 1917. Volume 22 Unit. 157th Field R E		
Heading	War Diary Of 157th. (Field) Company R.E. from 1st. September 1917 to 30th. September 1917		
War Diary	Hamelincourt	01/09/1917	30/09/1917

Diagram etc	Wiring Organisation		
Heading	War Diary For Month Of October, 1917. Unit 157th Field Coy RE Volume Number 23		
Heading	War Diary Of 157th. (Field) Company R.E. from 1st. October 1917 to 31st. October 1917		
War Diary	Hamelincourt	01/10/1917	31/10/1917
Heading	War Diary For Month Of November, 1917. Volume 24 Unit 157th Fld Coy RE		
War Diary	Hamelincourt	01/11/1917	30/11/1917
Operation(al) Order(s)	157th. (Field) Company R.E. Operation Order No. 1 of 19th November 1917	19/11/1917	19/11/1917
Heading	War Diary For Month Of December, 1917. Volume. 25 Unit. 157th Field Coy RE		
Heading	War Diary Of The 157th. (Field) Company R.E. from 1st. December 1917 to 31st. December 1917.		
War Diary	Hamelincourt	01/12/1917	31/12/1917
Heading	War Diary. For Month Of January, 1918. Volume. 26 Unit. 157th Fd Coy RE		
War Diary	Villers Faucon	01/01/1918	31/01/1918
Heading	War Diary For Month Of February, 1918. Volume 27 Unit. 157th Field Coy RE		
War Diary	Villers Faucon	01/02/1918	28/02/1918
Heading	16th Divisional Engineers 157th Field Company R.E. March 1918		
War Diary	Villers-Faucon	01/03/1918	21/03/1918
War Diary	Hamel	22/03/1918	23/03/1918
War Diary	Cappy	24/03/1918	26/03/1918
War Diary	Mericourt	27/03/1918	27/03/1918
War Diary	La Motte	28/03/1918	28/03/1918
War Diary	Hamel	29/03/1918	31/03/1918
Heading	War Diary Of The 157th (Field) Company R.E. From 1st. April 1918 to 30th. April 1918. Vol. 29		
War Diary	Aubigny	01/04/1918	03/04/1918
War Diary	Saleux	04/04/1918	05/04/1918
War Diary	Onicourt	06/04/1918	12/04/1918
War Diary	Woirel	13/04/1918	13/04/1918
War Diary	Ferrieres	14/04/1918	29/04/1918
War Diary	Isburgues	30/04/1918	30/04/1918
Heading	War Diary Of The 157th. (Field) Company R.E. From 1st. May 1918 to 31st. May 1918. Vol 30		
War Diary	Pecqueur 36A Sheet. 1.20.b.	01/05/1918	14/05/1918
War Diary	Pecqueur 36A I 10.b	15/05/1918	30/05/1918
War Diary	Coyecque	31/05/1918	31/05/1918
Heading	War Diary Of The 157th (Field) Company R.E. from 1st. June 1918 to 30th. June 1918 Vol 31		
War Diary	Coyecque Bourthes Calais 13.E.5.2.3	01/06/1918	04/06/1918
War Diary	Wicquinghem Calais 13	05/06/1918	08/06/1918
War Diary	Lacres Calais D.5.05.15	09/06/1918	16/06/1918
War Diary	Lacres D5.05.15	17/06/1918	30/06/1918
Heading	War Diary Of The 157th (Field) Company R.E. from 1st July 1918 to 31st. July 1918 Vol 32		
War Diary	Lacres Calais 13 5.d	01/07/1918	28/07/1918
War Diary	Hardelot Plage Calais 13	29/07/1918	31/07/1918
Heading	War Diary Of The 157th. (Field) Company R E. from 1st. August 1918 to 31st. August 1918. Vol 33		
War Diary	Hardelot Plage Calais 13. 5A	01/08/1918	02/08/1918

War Diary	Frencq Calais 13 (6 C 39.79)	03/08/1918	19/08/1918
War Diary	Bajus Lens II. F.1	20/08/1918	20/08/1918
War Diary	Sailly La Bourse	21/08/1918	21/08/1918
War Diary	Annequin F 23 D Central	22/08/1918	31/08/1918
Heading	War Diary Of The 157th. (Field) Company R.E. from 1st. September 1918 to 30th. September 1918 Vol 34		
War Diary	Annequin F 23d Cent.	01/09/1918	23/09/1918
War Diary	Sailly-Labourse L. 3.a.3.8	24/09/1918	29/09/1918
War Diary	Sailly-Labourse	30/09/1918	30/09/1918
War Diary	Sailly-Labourse. L 3a.3.8	01/10/1918	09/10/1918
War Diary	Annequin F 23d 94	05/10/1918	06/10/1918
War Diary	Auchy A 23d.1.3	07/10/1918	15/10/1918
War Diary	Billy Berclau	16/10/1918	16/10/1918
War Diary	Bauvin	17/10/1918	18/10/1918
War Diary	Pont-A-Marcq	18/10/1918	19/10/1918
War Diary	Templeuve	19/10/1918	21/10/1918
War Diary	Taintignies	22/10/1918	31/10/1918
War Diary	Taintignies (U 26C-Sheet 37)	01/11/1918	01/11/1918
War Diary	La Posterie (A 6 C-Sheet 44)	02/11/1918	07/11/1918
War Diary	Florent (U 25a-Sheet 37)	08/11/1918	08/11/1918
War Diary	Antoing (V 15d-Sheet 37)	09/11/1918	14/11/1918
War Diary	Antoing (V 15d-Sheet 37) And Pt. Rumes	15/11/1918	15/11/1918
War Diary	Pt. Rumes & Place Compte	16/11/1918	16/11/1918
War Diary	Place Compte & Rue De Moncheux	17/11/1918	17/11/1918
War Diary	Rue De Moncheux	18/11/1918	30/11/1918
Heading	War Diary Of The 157th (Field) Company R.E-From 1st December 1918 To 31st December 1918 Vol 37		
War Diary	Attiches	01/12/1918	31/12/1918
Heading	War Diary Of The 157th (Field) Company R.E. From 1st. January 1919 To 31st January 1919 Vol 38		
War Diary	Attiches	01/01/1919	31/01/1919
Heading	War Diary Of The 157th Field Coy RE from 1st February 1919 31st February 1919 Vol 39		
War Diary	Attiches	01/02/1919	19/03/1919
War Diary	Attiches (France)	20/03/1919	29/03/1919
War Diary	Duren (Germany)	30/03/1919	30/03/1919
War Diary	Birciel (Germany)	31/03/1919	31/03/1919

(3)

WO 95 / 1965
16 Division
Headquarters Branches &
Services

Dec 1915 - March 1919

157 FIELD COMPANY ROYAL
ENGINEERS

16TH DIVISION

157TH FIELD COY R.E.
DEC 1915 - MAR 1919

157 ?? Co. R.E.
Dec.
vol. I

BEF 20.12.15

16 Dn

Dec 15
Mar 19

WAR DIARY
or
INTELLIGENCE SUMMARY

(Erase heading not required.)

Army Form C. 2118

Unit 157th Field Coy R.E.

Place	Date	Hour	Summary of Events and Information	Remarks and references to Appendices
Blackdown	19.12.15	2.0 a.m.	Company left for FARNBOROUGH Station.	
FARNBOROUGH	— " —	5.30 a.m.	½ Company entrained and left for SOUTHAMPTON	
— " —	— " —	6.35 a.m.	½ Company entrained and left for SOUTHAMPTON	
SOUTHAMPTON	— " —	3.30 p.m.	Company entrained and left for HAVRE on SS. "COURTFIELD"	
HAVRE	20.12.15	9.0 a.m.	Company disembarked and proceeded by march route to REST CAMP No 5 arriving at 4.0 p.m.	
— " —	21.12.15	8.0 a.m.	Left REST CAMP No 5 for POINT No 3 GARE DES MARCHANDISES, and entrained.	
— " —	21.12.15	12.0 n.	Left HAVRE and proceeded to CHOQUES via ROUEN, BUCHY, ABBEVILLE and St OMER.	
— " —			Halts at BUCHY and ABBEVILLE for coffee and hot water.	
CHOQUES	22.12.15	12.30 p.m.	Left CHOQUES by march route for MAZINGARBE	
MAZINGARBE	— " —	7.0 p.m.	Arrived at MAZINGARBE and were accommodated in Huts. Reported to C.R.E. 1st Division attached to 1st Division for work.	
— " —	23.12.15		Settled down in Huts, received instructions as to work for next day. (Strong points at QUALITY STREET)	
— " —	24.12.15		Company employed in preparing "Strong Points" at QUALITY STREET Xmas Day. No work done. Church Parade at 12.0 noon.	
— " —	25.12.15			
— " —	26.12.15		Company employed on "Strong Points" at QUALITY STREET. 1 N.C.O admitted to hospital	
— " —	27.12.15		Company employed on "Strong Points" at QUALITY STREET. One mule died (note).	
— " —		11.0 a.m.	Interpreter reported for duty	

WAR DIARY
or
INTELLIGENCE SUMMARY

Army Form C. 2118

Unit 157th Field Coy R.E.

Place	Date	Hour	Summary of Events and Information	Remarks and references to Appendices
MAZINGARBE	28.12.15	10.30 a.m.	Lecture arranged by H.Q. 16th Div. to 20 officers and N.C.Os of the Company on gas helmets and protection against gas attack.	
"	29.12.15		Company employed on "Strong Points" at QUALITY STREET. 2 Sections employed on "Strong Points" at QUALITY STREET. 2 Sections employed on wire entanglement in front of RESERVE TRENCH working with 26th Field Coy R.E. 1 N.C.O admitted to hospital	
"	"	9.30 p.m.	Orders from C.R.E. to send 2 sections to BOMY on 31.12.15 (via AMETTES)	
"	30.12.15	8.0 a.m.	Nos 2 and 4 sections left for AMETTES en route for BOMY. Nos 1 and 3 Sections employed on wire entanglement "Strong Points" at QUALITY STREET	
"	31.12.15		Nos 1 and 3 Sections employed on wire entanglement in RESERVE TRENCH	

Will afent
Capt. 157th Field Coy R.E.
O.C. 157th

157th F.C. R.E.
Vol 2

WAR DIARY
or
INTELLIGENCE SUMMARY
(Erase heading not required.)

Unit 157th Fd Coy RE   Army Form C. 2118

Place	Date	Hour	Summary of Events and Information	Remarks and references to Appendices
MAZINGARBE	1.1.16		Nos 1 and 3 Section employed on wire entanglement in front of RESERVE TRENCH assisted by 20 Pioneers.	
"	2.1.16		Rest. (men to have feet being knocked up by them long march to and from work)	
			1 N.C.O admitted to hospital	
			1 N.C.O. returned to duty from hospital.	
"	3.1.16	6.15am	Order received to effect that from 4.1.16 the company would be administered by 1st Div.	To replace mule which died 27.12.15
"			Order received to draw 1 mule from South IRISH HORSE.	
"			Nos 1 and 3 Sections employed on wire entanglement in front of RESERVE TRENCH (assisted by 90 Pioneers)	
"		8.50pm	Order received from 1st Div to draw rations from 1st Div Refilling Point.	
"	4.1.16		1 N.C.O returned to duty from hospital	
"			Nos 1 and 3 Sections employed on wire entanglement in front RESERVE TRENCH (assisted by 90 Pioneers)	
"	5.1.16		1 N.C.O admitted to hospital	
"			4 men Sent away to receive dental treatment	
"			Nos 1 and 3 sections employed on "Strong Point" at QUALITY STREET.	
"	6.1.16		"Lieut F.H. MONCKTON admitted to hospital (sick)	
"			Nos 1 and 3 Sections employed on "Strong Point" at QUALITY STREET	
"	7.1.16		Nos 1 and 3 Sections employed on "Strong Point" at QUALITY STREET	
"	8.1.16		Nos 1 and 3 Sections employed on "Strong Point" at QUALITY STREET	
"	9.1.16		1 Sapper admitted to hospital	
"			Nos 1 and 3 Sections employed on "Strong Point" at QUALITY STREET	

Army Form C. 2118

WAR DIARY
157th Fd Coy RE
or
INTELLIGENCE SUMMARY
(Erase heading not required.)

Instructions regarding War Diaries and Intelligence Summaries are contained in F. S. Regs., Part II. and the Staff Manual respectively. Title Pages will be prepared in manuscript.

Place	Date	Hour	Summary of Events and Information	Remarks and references to Appendices
MAZINGARBE	10.1.16		2 Sappers admitted to Hospital. No 1 Section assisted 26th Fd Coy RE in laying on Water Supply to RESERVE TRENCH. No 3 Section employed on "STRONG POINTS" at QUALITY STREET.	
-"-	11.1.16	2.30	C.R.E. and Adjutant visited 157th Coy BillB.	
-"-	-"-	3.0	Church Service	
-"-	-"-		No 1 Section again assisted 26th Fd Coy R.E. No 3 Section employed on STRONG POINTS at QUALITY STREET. 1 Sapper in No 1 Section wounded by shell burst	
-"-	12.1.16	6pm	Lieut MONCKTON returned to duty from Hospital. 1 NCO returned to duty from Hospital. Inspection of Gas Helmets. Nos 1 and 3 Sections employed on "STRONG POINTS" at QUALITY STREET	
-"-	-"-	Sep		
-"-	-"-			
-"-	13.1.16		MARROW. 1 Sapper returned to duty from Hospital. Company employed on fatigue round trenches, no injuries. Nos 1 and 3 Sections employed on "STRONG POINTS" at QUALITY STREET	
-"-	14.1.16		Nos 1 and 3 Sections employed on "STRONG POINTS" at QUALITY STREET	
-"-	15.1.16		1 Sapper returned to duty from Hospital	
-"-	16.1.16		Nos 1 and 3 Sections employed on "STRONG POINTS" at QUALITY STREET	

Army Form C. 2118

157th Fd Coy R.E.

WAR DIARY
or
INTELLIGENCE SUMMARY

(Erase heading not required.)

Place	Date	Hour	Summary of Events and Information	Remarks and references to Appendices
MAZINGARBE	17.1.16		4 Sappers returned from Hospital for duty. (3 dental cases)	
"	18.1.16		Nos 1 and 3 Section employed on "Strong Points" at QUALITY STREET. Nos 1 and 3 Sections employed on "Strong Points" at QUALITY STREET. D.A.A.Q.M.G. and A.D.V.S. 16th Div. visited Stables. Interpreter changed.	
"	19.1.16		A.D.V.S. 15th Div. visited Stables. 1 Sapper returned to duty from hospital. Nos 1 & 3 Sections employed on "Strong Points" at QUALITY STREET.	
"	20.1.16		C.R.E. & adjutant 16th Div Engineers visited 157th Fd Coy. 2nd Lt. J. H. MONCKTON promoted Lieutenant, antedated to 23.5.15"	
"	-		Nos 1 & 3 Sections employed on "Strong Points" at QUALITY STREET	
"	21.1.16		1 Sapper admitted to Hospital. 1 Sapper returned to duty from Hospital. Rest Day from night work. Coy attended Baths. Sections employed on improving Stable accommodation.	
"	22.1.16		Sections employed on "Strong Points" at QUALITY STREET.	

Army Form C. 2118

WAR DIARY
or
INTELLIGENCE SUMMARY

157th Fd Coy RE

(Erase heading not required.)

Instructions regarding War Diaries and Intelligence Summaries are contained in F.S. Regs., Part II. and the Staff Manual respectively. Title Pages will be prepared in manuscript.

Place	Date	Hour	Summary of Events and Information	Remarks and references to Appendices
MAZINGARBE	23.1.16	4.15pm	5.9 Shells fell near Stables and mess huts. 1 mounted N.C.O wounded and removed to hospital. One driver and Cpl M.C.O very slightly wounded (at duty again). 2nd Lt G CARLYLE RE wounded and removed to hospital. Nos 1 and 3 Sections employed on "Strong Points" at QUALITY STREET.	
"	24.1.16		Nos 1 and 3 Sections employed on "Strong Points at QUALITY STREET. Party also employed during the day on sandbagging round walls of huts (at MAZINGARBE)	
"	25.1.16		Capt R S ASHER removed to hospital suffering from Shellshock. Nos 1 & 3 Sections employed on Strong Points at QUALITY STREET. Party also employed during the day on Sand bagging round walls of huts.	
		2.0pm	Inspection of Gasbelmets, iron rations, field dressings.	
		3.0pm	Church Service.	
"	26.1.16	1.0pm	C.R.E. visited 157th Fd Coy RE, bringing Lieut GREENHOW to report for duty.	
"			No 1 Section assisted 173rd Fd Coy RE in cutting down trees on LENS Road & right.	
"			Nos 2 & 3 Sections employed on "Strong Points" at QUALITY STREET. Party also employed during the day on sandbagging round walls of huts.	
"	27.1.16	9.30pm	Vet Officer 16th Div Examined Horses and Mules of H.Q Section.	
"			Nos 1 and 3 Sections employed all day on Sand bagging round walls of huts. Rest day from night work.	
"		6.15pm	Order received that enemy was attacking. Coy to stand by until further orders.	
"		7.15pm	" " all into quiet. Order to stand by cancelled.	

1875 Wt. W593/826 1,000,000 4/15 J.B.C. & A. A.D.S.S./Forms/C. 2118.

Army Form C. 2118

WAR DIARY
or
INTELLIGENCE SUMMARY

157th Fd Coy RE

(Erase heading not required.)

Instructions regarding War Diaries and Intelligence Summaries are contained in F.S. Regs., Part II. and the Staff Manual respectively. Title Pages will be prepared in manuscript.

Place	Date	Hour	Summary of Events and Information	Remarks and references to Appendices
MAZINGARBE	28.1.16	9.0 am	Vet. officer 16th Div. visited stables and mallinjal horses and mules of Nos 1 and 3 Sections. Nos 1 and 3 Sections assisted by Infantry Working Party (100) employed at QUALITY STREET on communication trenches between offensive works. Work interrupted by gasshells.	
" —	29.1.16		Nos 1 and 3 Sections assisted by Infantry Working Party employed at QUALITY STREET on Communication Trenches & defensive works.	
" —	30.1.16		Nos 1 and 3 Sections assisted by Infantry Working Party employed at QUALITY STREET on Communication Trenches and defensive works. 1 N.C.O. admitted to hospital	
" —	31.1.16		Received notice that 2 officers were on their way as reinforcements. Nos 1 and 3 Sections assisted by Infantry Working Party employed at QUALITY STREET on Communication Trenches & defensive works.	

Henn of Goff
Capt. & fdCoy RE.
O.C. 157

157th F.C.R.E.
16   vol: 3

WAR DIARY
or
INTELLIGENCE SUMMARY

(Erase heading not required.)

Army Form C. 2118

157th Field Coy RE

Place	Date	Hour	Summary of Events and Information	Remarks and references to Appendices
MAZINGARBE	1.2.16	12.30pm	CRE and Adjutant 164 Div' Engineers visited Coy bringing with them the following officers as reinforcements :— 2nd Lieut F.J. COLLEY RE. 2nd Lieut H.M. SIMMS RE. Nos 1 and 3 sections employed on works of defence at QUALITY STREET by night. Inspection of gas helmets, field dressings, iron rations	
"	2.2.16	3.0pm	1 Sapper admitted to hospital Lecture by M.O. on First Aid. Sections employed by day on protecting walls of hut with sand bags. No night work.	
"	3.2.16	3.0pm	1 Sapper admitted to hospital Nos 1 and 3 sections with Infantry working party employed on defensive works at QUALITY STREET by night. Nos 1 and 3 sections employed by day on protecting walls of hut with sand bags.	
"	4.2.16		M. BRIGAUT, Interpreter left Company. Nos 1 and 3 Sections employed by night on defensive works at QUALITY STREET with an Infantry working party.	
"	5.2.16	2.30pm	Nos 1 and 3 sections employed by night on defensive works at QUALITY STREET with Infantry working party. Lecture on First Aid by M.O.	

WAR DIARY or INTELLIGENCE SUMMARY

157th Fd Coy RE

Army Form C. 2118

(Erase heading not required.)

Place	Date	Hour	Summary of Events and Information	Remarks and references to Appendices
MAZINGARBE	6.2.16	11.0am	O.C. left to visit Nos 2 and 4 Sections at AMETTES. These two Sections had been employed in RE work in connection with Back Billets. Erecting Bath house, stables, sheds for motor cars etc.	
			Nos 1 and 3 Sections employed by night on defensive works at QUALITY STREET, with an Infantry Working Party.	
			1 Driver admitted to hospital	
	RAINE		New P.H. gas helmet drill.	
			Gas helmet issued & inspected.	
	7.2.16	11.0am	Gas helmet drill.	
			Nos 1 and 3 sections employed by night on defensive works at QUALITY STREET.	
	8.2.16		Nos 1 and 3 Sections employed by night on defensive works at QUALITY STREET.	
	9.2.16	1.0pm	O.C. returned from AMETTES.	
			Message received to effect that 157 Coy Two Sections would move from MAZINGARBE to L'ECLEME	
			Billeting en route at HOCHIN on 13.2.16.	
		7.30pm	Lieut GREENHOW left for AMETTES to return to his Section.	
			1 Driver returned to duty from hospital	
			Nos 1 and 3 Section employed by night on defensive works at QUALITY STREET, with Infantry Working Party.	
	10.2.16		Nos 1 and 3 Sections employed by night on defensive works at QUALITY STREET, with Infantry Working Party.	
	11.2.16	6.30am	Showed O.C. 91st Coy RE round the lines at QUALITY STREET, and arranged for him to take over on 12.2.16	
		12/16	1 Sapper admitted as sick to Field Army for 155 Coy RE from No 2 Section, attached until move to HQ 9/16/9	
		1.30	Received transport "Gas Alert" from 15th Division. Inspected helmets at 2.30pm	

WAR DIARY 157ᵗʰ Field Coy. R.E. Army Form C. 2118

Intelligence Summary (Erase heading not required.)

Place	Date	Hour	Summary of Events and Information	Remarks and references to Appendices
MAZINGARBE	11.2.16		Nos 1 and 3 Sections employed by night on defensive works at QUALITY STREET with Welshmen Mining Bn.	
--	12.2.16		1 Sapper admitted to hospital. Scout Oates received travelling persons orders re move. Company moves to AMETTES	
--	13.2.16	10.30a	On 14.2.16, Personnel by train to LILLERS transport by road. Company employed in loading sappers & preparing for move.	
--	14.2.16		Company preparing for move, clearing billets, loading wagons etc. Road for transport reconnoitred. Orders issued for move.	
--			Transport of Coy left MAZINGARBE at 8.0 a.m. and arrived at AMETTES at 3.30 p.m. Personnel of Coy. left MAZINGARBE at 9.30 a.m., entrained at NOEUX LES MINES for LILLERS, Marched to AMETTES arriving at 4.15 p.m. Billets had been arranged by Nos 2 & 4 Sections who were already billeted in AMETTES.	
AMETTES		6 p.m	Received order that G.O.C. would inspect the Coy on 17.2.15 at 3.30 p.m.	
--	15.2.16		Nos 2 & 4 Sections carried on with work they had in hand (infantry billet accommodation in neighbourhood) Nos 1 and 3 Sections at Head Qrs employed in cleaning up their billets, unloading & packing waggons, cleaning harness etc.	

157th FIELD COMPANY Army Form C. 2118
R.E.

WAR DIARY
or
INTELLIGENCE SUMMARY
(Erase heading not required.)

Place	Date	Hour	Summary of Events and Information	Remarks and references to Appendices
METTES	15.2.16	2.30pm	A.D.M.S. inspected all horses & mules.	
— " —	16.2.16		Company employed as on 15.2.16.	
		2.30pm	Parade in marching order. Rifle exercises.	
		7.30pm	Message received that G.O.C's Inspection on 17.2.16 was cancelled.	
— " —	17.2.16		Company employed as on 15.2.16 also	
		11 a.m.	Parade in Marching order. Rifle exercises.	
— " —	18.2.16		Company employed as on 15.2.16	
		2.30pm	Parade for Rifle Exercises.	
		1.0pm	Message received that G.O.C. will inspect the Coy at 11.0am on 19.2.16	
— " —	19.2.16	11.0am	Inspection by G.O.C. 16th Division.	
			Company employed in afternoon as on 15.2.16.	
— " —	20.2.16	5.0pm	Rest day. Message received from O.C. to report at H.Q. 49th Bde at 9.0 am 21/2/16	
— " —	21.2.16	9.0am	O.C. reported at H.Qrs 49th Brigade.	
			No 1 Section took over R.E. Works	
			Nos 2, 3 & 4 Section training under Section Officers.	
— " —	22.2.16	11 am	1 N.C.O. joined as reinforcement	
			No 1 Section & H.Q'rs on R.E. works	
			No 2, 3, 4 Section training under Section Officers.	

WAR DIARY or INTELLIGENCE SUMMARY

Army Form C. 2118

157th Field Coy RE

(Erase heading not required.)

Place	Date	Hour	Summary of Events and Information	Remarks and references to Appendices
GOMETTES	23.2.16		No 1 Section and Head Quarters employed on RE works.	
		2.30pm	Nos 2, 3 & 4 Sections Training under Section Officers.	
			Orders received to stand by to move to IIIrd Corps area on 25th or 26th Feb.	
		3.0pm	Orders received cancelling above.	
	24.2.16		1 Light Draft Horse & one riding horse drawn from remounts to complete mounted establishment.	
			No 1 Section and Head Quarters employed on RE works.	
			Nos 2, 3 & 4 Sections Training under Section Officers.	
		8.30pm	Orders received that 157th Field Coy would be required to move, with No a Inf Bde, to new billets area on 26.2.16.	
	25.2.16	10.15am	Verbal orders received from CRE cancelling above orders.	
			Company employed on packing up and in finishing off works on hand.	
		1.30pm	Orders received to be prepared to move on 28.2.16.	
		2.30pm	O.C. went to BETHUNE for conference on Trench Mortars.	
	26.2.16	9.15am	Orders received for Company to move to LES HARISOIRS on 29.2.16	
			Company employed on packing up and in finishing off works on hand.	
			Nos. 2 and 3 Sections sent to assist transport of 49th Inf Bde who were moving to new billeting area.	
		3.0pm	Horses received that a motor lorry had stuck in ditch near MSDON. No 2 Section went out and got it on to the road.	
	27.2.16	9.0am	C.R.E. & H.Q. 1st Army RE left for BUSNES	
			Company employed as on 26.2.16	
	28.2.16		Company employed as on 26.2.16. No 1 Section erecting Stables at ST HILLIARE	
		2.30pm	Orders received ordering Company to move to LA MIQUELLERIE on 29.2.16	

WAR DIARY or INTELLIGENCE SUMMARY

157th Field Coy RE Army Form C. 2118

(Erase heading not required.)

Instructions regarding War Diaries and Intelligence Summaries are contained in F. S. Regs., Part II. and the Staff Manual respectively. Title Pages will be prepared in manuscript.

Place	Date	Hour	Summary of Events and Information	Remarks and references to Appendices
AMETTES	24.2.16	10.30am	Company left for LA MIGUELERIE	
LA MIQUELLERIE		1.30pm	Company arrived & settled into Billets.	

MWMacBeng
Capt RE
O.C. 157th Fd Coy RE

LETTERS

Vol 4

WAR DIARY
or
INTELLIGENCE SUMMARY

(Erase heading not required.)

157th Field Coy R E

Army Form C. 2118

Place	Date	Hour	Summary of Events and Information	Remarks and references to Appendices
LA MIQUELLRIE	1.3.16		No 2 section employed in erecting Motor Garage at H.Q. 16th Div. Remainder of Coy employed on cleaning up billets, improving stable accommodation etc.	
"	2.3.16		Company employed on works served the billets and training under Section Officers. One Sergeant regained the company from Survey Company	
"	3.3.16		Company employed as on 2.3.16.	
		9.30 am	Vet. officer inspected all horses 9 mules.	
"	4.3.16		Company employed on RE Works. Order received that Company would move tomorrow & be attached to 15th Division for work.	
		2.15 pm	Order received cancelling above. Company to move tomorrow to be attached to 12th Division, to be billeted at ANNEQUIN	
		9.15 pm		
"	5.3.16	9.0 am	Company left LA MIQUELLERIE	
ANNEQUIN		3.30 pm	Company arrived & billeted	
"	6.3.16		O.C. visited turnks 9 craters by HOHENZOLLERN Redoubt to be taken over for work. Company settled into billets, fixed up staff etc. 5 Reinforcements arrived (1 corpl 4 sappers 1 pioneer) Company working by day on craters # 4, B and C and WEST FACE Trench	
"	7.3.16		Work taken over from 70th Company, under CRE 12th Division, in conjunction with 37th Brigade) Casualties 1 Sapper killed (wounded for of time on Sight, kept at dark). All in C crater Lieut COLLEY slightly wounded and suffering from severe shock	

Army Form C. 2118

WAR DIARY
or
INTELLIGENCE SUMMARY 157th Field Coy R.E.
(Erase heading not required.)

Place	Date	Hour	Summary of Events and Information	Remarks and references to Appendices
ANNEQUIN	8.3.16		Lieut COLLEY removed to hospital	
			No.4 Section working in 'C' Crater in morning	
			German attack stopped night working parties	
	9.3.16		Work on 'C' 'B' & No.4 Craters handed over to 87th Field Company & No.3 CRATER	
			Company employed on NORTHAMPTON TRENCH by day, and on WEST FACE and No.3 CRATER by night. Assisted by 1 Platoon Pioneers	
	10.3.16		Company employed as on 9th inst. Assisted by 1 Platoon Pioneers	
	11.3.16		Company employed as on 9th inst. Assisted by 1 Platoon Pioneers & 2 Platoons 9 DUBLINS	
	12.3.16		Company employed on NORTHAMPTON TRENCH by day and on WEST FACE and No.3 CRATER by night. Assisted by 1 Platoon Pioneers & 2 Coys DUBLINS.	
			CRE & adjutant 16th Div'n visited Company	
	13.3.16		Company employed on NORTHAMPTON TRENCH by day and on WEST FACE and No.3 CRATER by night. Assisted by 1 Platoon Pioneers and 2 Coys DUBLINS.	
		8 p.m.	Message received stating that Company will rejoin 16th Div'n on 16.3.16.	
		6.15 p.m.	1/Lt BLACK R.E. joined as a reinforcement	

WAR DIARY or INTELLIGENCE SUMMARY

Army Form C. 2118

157th Field Company RE

(Erase heading not required.)

Place	Date	Hour	Summary of Events and Information	Remarks and references to Appendices
ANNEQUIN	14.3.16		Company employed on NORTHAMPTON TRENCH by day, and on WEST FACE and CRATER No 3 by night, assisted by 3 Platoons of Infantry and 1 Platoon Pioneers.	
		11.0 a.m.	Message received stating that Company will move to CAUCHY-A-LA-TOUR on 16/3/16	
	15.3.16		1 Section R.E. employed on NORTHAMPTON TRENCH by day. Company prepared for move.	
CAUCHY A LA TOUR	16.3.16	8.30 a.m.	Company left for CAUCHY A LA TOUR	
		3.30 p.m.	Company arrived and settled into new billets	
	17.3.16		Company employed in cleaning up new billets stables etc. Message from Corps Commander re good work done by all troops engaged on work round the HOHENZOLLERN REDOUBT read out on parade.	
	18.3.16		Section training under Section officers	
	19.3.16		Bliss Rest day.	
	20.3.16		Sections training under Section officers.	
	21.3.16		Section training under Section officers. 3 N.C.O's and men returned from Div. Grenade School. O.C. received orders to proceed to 73rd Coy RE MAZINGARBE on 22nd inst. & return on 25th inst.	
	22.3.16		O.C. proceeded to MAZINGARBE. Sections training under section officers.	

WAR DIARY or INTELLIGENCE SUMMARY

157th Field Coy. R.E. Army Form C. 2118

(Erase heading not required.)

Instructions regarding War Diaries and Intelligence Summaries are contained in F. S. Regs., Part II. and the Staff Manual respectively. Title Pages will be prepared in manuscript.

Place	Date	Hour	Summary of Events and Information	Remarks and references to Appendices
CAUCHY-A-LATOUR	23.3.16		O.C. Lorry taken over from 73rd Coy. returned to 157th F'd Coy. Sections employed under Section Officers	
"		5.0 pm	Orders received for Company to move on 27.3.16 to takeover billets from 74th & 74 Coy R.E (PHILOSOPHE) Billeting party	
"	24.3.16		Sections employed under Section Officers 26.3.16	
"		11.30 pm	Orders received for Lt SIMMS to proceed to MAZINGARBE on 25/3/16 to take over & inspect M.G. Emplacements from Pioneer Battalion 15th Divn	
"	25.3.16	10.0 am	Lt SIMMS left for MAZINGARBE. Sections employed under Section Officers	
"	26.3.16	8.15 am	left & 2 Sappers left for PHILOSOPHE as Billeting party	
"		10.0 am	C.R.E. arrived to explain work to be done on arrival in new area	
"			Company employed on packing up.	
"	27.3.16	8.0 am	Dismounted portion left & entrained at NOEUX LES MINES, marched to PHILOSOPHE, arriving 12.30.	
"		8.30 am	Transport & mounted portion left, and arrived at PHILOSOPHS at 2.0 pm Billeted at MAZINGARBE.	
PHILOSOPHE		4.30 pm	C.R.E. 16th Div visited Coy.	
"	29.3.16		Company employed as Reserve Company. Work consisting of Machine Gun Emplacements, maintenance of Tramways, protected killets with steel shelters, water supply, odd jobs for Town Major etc.	

WAR DIARY or INTELLIGENCE SUMMARY

157th Field Coy R.E. Army Form C. 2118

(Erase heading not required.)

Place	Date	Hour	Summary of Events and Information	Remarks and references to Appendices
PHILOSOPHE	29.3.16		Company employed as on 28.3.16	
"	30.3.16		Company employed as on 28.3.16	
"	31.3.16		Company employed as on 28.3.16	

Hunnerford
Capt. R.E.
O.C. 157th Field Coy R.E.

Army Form C. 2118
XVI   157th Field Coy R.E. Vol 5

WAR DIARY or INTELLIGENCE SUMMARY
(Erase heading not required.)

Place	Date	Hour	Summary of Events and Information	Remarks and references to Appendices
PHILOSOPHE	1.4.16		Company in Reserve. 1 Section employed on concrete M.G. emplacements Nos 1 & 2 in front of VILLAGE LINE near CHALK PIT ALLEY (night work) 1 Section employed on maintenance & installation of tramway from VICTORIA to POSEN STATION. (mostly night work) 1 Section employed on erecting steel shelters in tonnes in PHILOSOPHE, maintenance of LENS Road between PHILOSOPHE Cross roads and FOSSE No 7, keeping communication trenches up to TENTH AVENUE in good order. 1 Section employed on odd jobs, such as emptying 16th Div Bomb Store, erecting Latrines for Town Major, painting notice boards, also strengthening cellar in Lett Bn. H.Qrs etc etc. 1 unarmoured Coy as a reinforcement.	
"	2.4.16		Company employed as above. C.R.E. & O.C. reconnoitred ground for running two new communication trenches up to TENTH AVENUE.	
"	3.4.16		Company employed as on 1.4.16.	

WAR DIARY or INTELLIGENCE SUMMARY

Army Form C. 2118

157th Field Coy. R.E.

(Erase heading not required.)

Place	Date	Hour	Summary of Events and Information	Remarks and references to Appendices
PHILOSOPHE	4.4.16		Company employed on same work as on 1.4.16	
"	5.4.16		do	
"	6.4.16		do	
			Routes for New communication trenches reconnoitred by O.C. & Brigadier 48th Inf. Bde.	
"	7.4.16		Company employed as on 1.4.16.	
		1.30 p.m	7 Men arrived as reinforcements. 5 Sappers 2 Pioneers	
"	8.4.16		Company employed as on 1.4.16	
			New communication trench started from 10th AVENUE via LONE TRENCH.	
"	9.4.16		Front line work Taken over from 156 Coy R.E in Left sector TULLOCH ROAD to POSEN ALLEY (exclusive). 47th Infantry Bde in the line	
			No.1 Section, work on listening galleries in front line near KINGSWAY	
			No.2 Section, work on Consolidation of craters E & J HAY ALLEY	
			No 3 Section, work on M.G. Dug outs in Reserve line & Support Line	
			No 4 Section work on M.G. Dug outs & Infantry Dug outs in Reserve Line & Support line (assisted by Bn Pioneers)	
			2 N.C.Os & 32 men from Infantry arrived to be attached for work with No 1 Section.	

WAR DIARY or INTELLIGENCE SUMMARY

Army Form C. 2118

157th Field Coy. R.E.

Instructions regarding War Diaries and Intelligence Summaries are contained in F.S. Regs., Part II. and the Staff Manual respectively. Title Pages will be prepared in manuscript.

(Erase heading not required.)

Place	Date	Hour	Summary of Events and Information	Remarks and references to Appendices
PHILOSOPHE	10.4.16		Company employed as on 9/4/16	
"	11.4.16		Company employed ~~...~~ Also new Bryan from Support trench to firing line S. of MAY ALLEY deepened.	
"	12.4.16		Company employed as on 9/4/16. 1 N.C.O. killed and one sapper wounded by Rifle Grenade while consolidating crater. A new Bryan from Support trench to front line N. of MAY ALLEY commenced.	
"	13.4.16		Company employed as on 9/4/16. 1 N.C.O. killed by Rifle Grenade while consolidating crater.	
"	14.4.16		Section employed on M.G. emplacements withdrawn and employed on front line making shelters for sentries.	
"	15.4.16		Company employed as on 14.4.16.	
"	16.4.16		Company employed as on 14.4.16. Very little work done in front line owing to enemy's trench mortar attack. Nos 1 Section continued work as usual on listening galleries. No. 4 " " " " Dug outs	
"	17.4.16		Nos 2 & 3 sections	
"	18.4.16		Work continued on improving front line technical craters, erecting shelters in front line near BROADWAY, and on Dug outs & listening galleries	
"	19.4.16		Work as on 15.4.16. Three Sappers arrived as reinforcements	

WAR DIARY or INTELLIGENCE SUMMARY

(Erase heading not required.)

Army Form C. 2118

157ᵃ Field Coy RE

Instructions regarding War Diaries and Intelligence Summaries are contained in F.S. Regs., Part II. and the Staff Manual respectively. Title Pages will be prepared in manuscript.

Place	Date	Hour	Summary of Events and Information	Remarks and references to Appendices
PHILOSOPHE	20.4.16		Work on 18.4.16 — 47ᵗʰ Infantry Bⁿ relieved by 49ᵗʰ Infʸ Bⁿ in left subsection.	
"	21.4.16		1 Driver wounded in billets.	
"	22.4.16		Work as on 18.4.16 with addition of an artillery O.P. being constructed in Reserve Line near VENDIN ALLEY	
"	23.4.16	2.30	Work as on 21.4.16. Each section on dugouts — one continues on mining galleries	
"	24.4.16		work as on 23.4.16	
"	25.4.16		" " 24.4.16	
"	26.4.16		" " 25.4.16. 2 Reinforcements reported (Mounted men)	
"	27.4.16		Work as on 26.4.16	
"	28.4.16		German gas attack about 4 am — 15 men gassed returning from dug-out work 1 & 2 sections cleary out front trenches sent by 1ˢᵗ Army minen werf.	
"	29.4.16		further German attack going with gas — Heard of death of 1st/5ʰ/Hero? gas, received on 28.4.16; sections engaged in making concealed entanglements & transporting & dumping to new front line.	
"	30.4.16		Quiet day — sections clearing ESSEX LANE, BERRY LANE, SUPPORT LINE and STRAW ALLEY.	
"	1.5.16		Quiet day — sections started work on Shakespeare Nʳ 1 Subsection Nʳ 2 O.P. August.	

HMcaeJeffᵀ
Capt RE
O.C. 157ᵃ Fd Coy RE

Army Form C. 2118

157 Field Coy R.E.
XVI VOL 6

WAR DIARY
or
INTELLIGENCE SUMMARY
(Erase heading not required.)

Instructions regarding War Diaries and Intelligence Summaries are contained in F.S. Regs., Part II. and the Staff Manual respectively. Title Pages will be prepared in manuscript.

Place	Date	Hour	Summary of Events and Information	Remarks and references to Appendices
PHILOSOPHE	1/5/16		Quiet day. Sections started Unusual work. No 1 S/ Shelter proofs, Nos 2, 3 & 4 Dugouts	
	2/5/16		NORMAL – Work on 1/5/16	
	3/5/16		Normal work as 2/5/16	
	4/5/16		Normal work as 3/5/16	
	5/5/16		Normal work as 4/5/16	
	6/5/16		Normal work as on 5/5/16	
	7/5/16		Handed over work to 155th Field Coy R.E.	
	8/5/16		Company in Reserve. No 1 Section employed on repair & maintenance of Tramways. No 2 Section employed on Infantry roads. No 3 Section employed on M.G. emplacements (concrete) near CHALKPIT ALLEY & on water supply at POSEN WELL. P.S & Dugouts near CHALK PIT ALLEY & 65 METRE POINT. No 2 Section employed on 8/5/16.	
	9/5/16		Work on on 8/5/16. Route for New Communication Trench through QUALITY STREET & then N of LENS Road to LOOS reconnoitred	
	10/5/16		Work on on 9/5/16. Route for New Communication Trench via LONDON ROAD, SOUTHERN UP, NORTH ST. to LOOS reconnoitred	

WAR DIARY
or
INTELLIGENCE SUMMARY
(Erase heading not required.)

Army Form C. 2118

157 Field Coy RE

Place	Date	Hour	Summary of Events and Information	Remarks and references to Appendices
PHILOSOPHE	11/5/16		Work as on 10/5/16. Also Infantry shown work to be done on new communication Trench 61.00s via LONDON ROAD.	
	12/5/16		Block of company very heavy shelled with 8 in Howitzer shells during afternoon and evening until about 8.0 p.m.	
			Work as on 11/5/16. Infantry started new communication Trench	
	13/5/16		Work as on 12/5/16	
	14/5/16		Work as on 13/5/16	
	15/5/16		Work as on 14/5/16	
	16/5/16		Work as on 15/5/16	
	17/5/16		Work as on 16/5/16	
			49th Inf Bde relieved 47th Inf Bde in Division right sector, taking over from 1st Division as far South as LENS Road.	
	18/5/16		2nd Lieut BOLTON arrived as a reinforcement	
			Work as on 17/5/16	
	19/5/16		Work as on 18/5/16	
			One Sergt & one L-Cpl wounded	
	20/5/16		Work as on 19/5/16	
	21/5/16		Work taken over from 156th Field Company in Loos Sector	

WAR DIARY or INTELLIGENCE SUMMARY

157th Field Coy R.E. Army Form C. 2118

(Erase heading not required.)

Instructions regarding War Diaries and Intelligence Summaries are contained in F. S. Regs., Part II. and the Staff Manual respectively. Title Pages will be prepared in manuscript.

Place	Date	Hour	Summary of Events and Information	Remarks and references to Appendices
PHILOSOPHE	21/5/16		1 Section employed on improving the consolidation of HARTS & HARRISONS Craters. 1 Section employed on M.G. Emplacements. 2 Section employed on Dug outs in Support line	
	22/5/16		Work as above.	
	23/5/16		Work as on 22/5/16. 5 reinforcements arrived (one mounted)	
	24/5/16		Work as on 23/5/16	
	25/5/16		Work as on 24/5/16. 1 reinforcement arrived (dismounted)	
	26/5/16		Work as on 25/5/16	
	27/5/16		Work stopped. Coy employed on strengthening wire on Reservoirs	
	28/5/16		Ordinary work as on 26/5/16 resumed	
	29/5/16		Work as on 26/5/16 except No 3 Section which put five steps in HAY HILL	
	30/5/16		Nos 1 & 2 Section working on Dugouts. No 3 Section wiring & fire stepping HAY MARKET. No 4 Section working round HARTS and HARRISONS Craters	
	31/5/16		Ordinary Work as on 28/5/16 resumed	

WAR DIARY or INTELLIGENCE SUMMARY

157th Field Coy R.E. Vol 7 June

Army Form C. 2118

Place	Date	Hour	Summary of Events and Information	Remarks and references to Appendices
PHILOSOPHE	1.6.16		Company working with 49th Inf Bde in LOOS Section. No 1 Section & No 2 Section making Dug outs. No 3 Section constructing Machine Gun emplacements. No 4 Section working on defences of HARTS and HARRISONS craters	
"	2.6.16		Work as above. 48th Brigade relieved 49th Bde	
"	3.6.16		Work as above. 1 CSM and 1 Sergt rejoined the Company	
"	4.6.16		Work as on 3.6.16	
"	5.6.16		Work as on 4.6.16	
"	6.6.16		Work as on 5.6.16	
"	7.6.16		Work as on 6.6.16. 5 Sappers arrived as reinforcements.	
"	8.6.16		Nos 1 and 3 Sections moved to billets in LOOS, under Lt Monckton. Lieut Bolton, 2 NCOs & 8 Sappers were instructed in hydraulic pipe pushing for purposes of mining etc. Work as on 7.6.16.	
"	9.6.16		Work as on 8.6.16. Lt Bolton proceeded to LOOS	
"	10.6.16		Work as on 9.6.16	

WAR DIARY or INTELLIGENCE SUMMARY

157th Field Coy R.E.   Army Form C. 2118

(Erase heading not required.)

Place	Date	Hour	Summary of Events and Information	Remarks and references to Appendices
PHILOSOPHE	11.6.16		Work as on 10.6.16	
"	12.6.16		Work as on 11.6.16	
"	13.6.16		Work as on 12.6.16	
			5 Sappers arrived as reinforcements	
"	14.6.16		Work as on 13.6.16	
"	15.6.16		Work as on 14.6.16	
"	16.6.16		Work as on 15.6.16	
"	17.6.16		Work as on 16.6.16	
			47th Infantry Brigade relieved 48th Infantry Bde. in LOOS Sector	
"	18.6.16		Work as on 17.6.16	
"	19.6.16		Work as on 18.6.16	
"	20.6.16		Work as on 19.6.16. Nos 1 and 3 Sections returned from LOOS	
			Officers of 155th Field Coy R.E. went round work to take over.	
			155th Field Coy R.E. took over the work, & 157th Coy went into Reserve.	
"	21.6.16		Work taken on from 155 Coy :—	
			No 1 Section : Water supply, Dugouts in Village line	
			No 2 Section : Tramway, roads maintenance R.A.M.C. and posts in 10th AVENUE	
			No 3 Section M.G. emplacements in front of Village line	

Army Form C. 2118

157th Field Coy RE

WAR DIARY
or
INTELLIGENCE SUMMARY
(Erase heading not required.)

Instructions regarding War Diaries and Intelligence Summaries are contained in F. S. Regs., Part II. and the Staff Manual respectively. Title Pages will be prepared in manuscript.

Place	Date	Hour	Summary of Events and Information	Remarks and references to Appendices
PHILOSOPHE	21.6.16		Work cont:- No 4 Section. Dugouts in Village Line and Artillery O.P. in MAROC	
	22.6.16		Work as on 21.6.16	
	23.6.16		Work as on 22.6.16	
	24.6.16		Work as on 23.6.16	
	25.6.16		Orders from CRE not to work beyond the Village Line. No 3 Section rollabaum. No 3 Section employed on making a splinter proof shelter for mounted section & in strengthening trills.	
	26.6.16		Work as on 25.6.16. 1 Sapper wounded. 1 Coy of Yorks (Pioneers) attached for work. Employed on Deepening PREVITE PASSAGE.	
	27.6.16		Work as on 26.6.16 with exception of Yorks Pioneers who worked on LONDON ROAD.	
	28.6.16		Work as on 27.6.16. (No Pioneers available) 1 Reinforcement arrived. (Driver)	
	29.6.16		Work as on 28.6.16. 1 N.C.O & 14 Sappers proceeded to Divisional School for work.	
	30.6.16		Work as on 29.6.16.	

AWMacLeod
Capt RE. OC 157th Field Coy RE

Army Form C. 2118

WAR DIARY
or
INTELLIGENCE SUMMARY
(Erase heading not required.)

Instructions regarding War Diaries and Intelligence Summaries are contained in F. S. Regs., Part II. and the Staff Manual respectively. Title Pages will be prepared in manuscript.

Place	Date	Hour	Summary of Events and Information	Remarks and references to Appendices

1875 Wt. W593/826 1,000,000 4/15 J.B.C. & A. A.D.S.S./Forms/C. 2118.

W A R   D I A R Y

157th Field Coy
Royal Engrs

1st. July to 31st. July 1916.

VOLUME No. 8

WAR DIARY or **INTELLIGENCE SUMMARY**

Army Form C. 2118

157th Field Coy RE

Place	Date	Hour	Summary of Events and Information	Remarks and references to Appendices
PHILOSOPHE	1.7.16		Company in Reserve. Work being done on Dugouts & Aid Posts in Village Line, O.P. at MAROC, maintenance of Tramways, roads etc.	
	2.7.16		Work as on 1.7.16.	
	3.7.16		Work as on 2.7.16. Work of 156th Field Coy RE inspected in 14 Bis Sector preparatory to taking over on night 4/5th.	
	4.7.16		Nos 2 and 4 Sections took over billets in Xth AVENUE from 156th Fd Coy RE.	
	5.7.16		Work started in 14 Bis Sector with 48th Infantry Bde. All Sections working on Dugouts & No 3 Section also working with M.G. Coy. #2A were specially employed under CRE anointing Special RE Coy in front line.	
	6.7.16		Work as on 5.7.16. Heavy bombardment of trenches round CHALK PIT WOOD.	
	7.7.16		Nos 2 and 4 Sections enabled Infantry in repair of front line trenches round CHALK PIT WOOD. Nos 1 and 3 Section working on Dugouts & M.G. Emplacements	
	8.7.16		Work as on 7.7.16	
	9.7.16		Work as on 8.7.16	
	10.7.16		Work as on 9.7.16	
	11.7.16		48th Brigade relieved by 47th Bde in 14 Bis Sector	
	12.7.16		No 3 Section working with M.G. Coy & Trench Mortar emplacements Nos 1, 2 &4 on Dugouts. 3 Reinforcements joined company.	

WAR DIARY or INTELLIGENCE SUMMARY

157th Field Coy R.E.

Army Form C. 2118

(Erase heading not required.)

Place	Date	Hour	Summary of Events and Information	Remarks and references to Appendices
PHILOSOPHE	13.7.16		Work as on 12.7.16	
	14.7.16		Work as on 13.7.16. Work in front line superintended by R.E.O around CHALK PIT.	
	15.7.16		Work as on 14.7.16	
	16.7.16		Work as on 15.7.16. Orders received that Capt. STRADLING R.E. is to report on 18.7.16 to CRE to take over duties of Adjutant.	
	17.7.16		Work as on 16.7.16	
	18.7.16		Capt. STRADLING R.E. left Coy to take over duties of Adjutant. Work as on 17.7.16. Carrying parties stopped at night owing to raid by MUNSTERS.	
	19.7.16		Work as on 18.7.16. 2nd Lt M.G.J M'HAFFIE arrived as a reinforcement	
	20.7.16		Work as on 19.7.16 49th Infantry Bde took over area to North (Right Brigade area of 15th Division)	
	21.7.16		Work as on 20.7.16. Lieut Moncton taken to hospital (injury to leg). Informed by CRE that the company would remain in 148 B/S Sector until further orders. Work to be carried out under CRE & not under Brigadier. 3 Section to work up in the line and one back in Reserve.	
	22.7.16		Work as on 21.7.16. 48th Infy Bde relieved in LOOS Sector by 45th Division 49th Infy Bde took over new area to N. of VENDIN ALLEY from 15th Division	

WAR DIARY

157th Field Coy RE Army Form C. 2118

or

INTELLIGENCE SUMMARY

(Erase heading not required.)

Instructions regarding War Diaries and Intelligence Summaries are contained in F. S. Regs., Part II. and the Staff Manual respectively. Title Pages will be prepared in manuscript.

Place	Date	Hour	Summary of Events and Information	Remarks and references to Appendices
PHILOSOPHE	23.7.16		No 1 Section working in Right Sub Sector of 14 Bis Sector (Billeted in X AVENUE)	
			No 4 " " Left " " "	
			No 3 " " on M.G. & T.M. Emplacement (Billeted in X AVENUE)	
			No 2 " in Reserve.	
	24.7.16		Work as on 23.7.16.	
	25.7.16		Work as on 24.7.16	
	26.7.16		Work as on 25.7.16.	
			"L" J.W. LEAHY joined as a reinforcement	
	27.7.16		Work as on 26.7.16.	
	28.7.16		Work as on 27.7.16	
	29.7.16		Work as on 28.7.16	
			L. F.H. MONCKTON returned from hospital.	
			2 Sections of 215 Field Coy. arrived to work on Dug Outs in 14 Bis Sector	
	30.7.16		Work as on 29.7.16	
	31.7.16		Work as on 30.7.16	
			49th Infantry Bde relieved 147th Infantry Bde in 14 Bis Sector	

MMradley 8
Capt RE
O.C. 157 F Coy RE

WAR DIARY.

157th Field Bay R.E.

MONTH OF AUGUST, 1916.

VOLUME :- 9

WAR DIARY
or
INTELLIGENCE SUMMARY

157th Field Coy RE

Army Form C. 2118

(Erase heading not required.)

Place	Date	Hour	Summary of Events and Information	Remarks and references to Appendices
PHILOSOPHE	1.8.16		8 Sappers arrived as reinforcements. No 4 Section relieved No 1 Section in X^t AVENUE. Dispositions of Company as follows:—	
			X^t AVENUE: No 4 Section working in Left Subsection of 141 Bde Sector. No 3 " " on M.G. Emplacements, Dugouts, T.M. & S/Bn Gun Emplacements & dug outs.	
			In PHILOSOPHE: No 2 Section working in Right Subsection 141 Bde Sector. No 1 Section in Reserve (working in NORTHERN SAP redoubt)	
			49th Infantry Bde in the line. At a Conference presided over by CRE, was informed that 16th Division would take over a new area shortly. Probably from LE RUTOIRE ALLEY to S.P. LOOS. 157th Field Coy to work in 49th Inf. Bde area which would be approximately from POSEN ALLEY to CAMERON ALLEY.	
	2.8.16		Work as on 1.8.16	
	3.8.16		Work as on 2.8.16	
	4.8.16		Work as on 3.8.16	
			Bⁿ Relief in 141 Bde Sector	
	5.8.16		Work as on 4.8.16	

WAR DIARY 157th Field Coy R.E.

Army Form C. 2118

or

INTELLIGENCE SUMMARY

(Erase heading not required.)

Instructions regarding War Diaries and Intelligence Summaries are contained in F.S. Regs., Part II. and the Staff Manual respectively. Title Pages will be prepared in manuscript.

Place	Date	Hour	Summary of Events and Information	Remarks and references to Appendices
PHILOSOPHE	6.8.16		Work as on 5.8.16	
	7.8.16		No 2 Section moved into billets in Xth AVENUE. No 3 Section returned to PHILOSOPHE	
	8.8.16		Work as on 6.8.16. Battn Relief in 14 Bis SECTION	
	9.8.16		Work as on 7.8.16 except that No 4 Section was withdrawn to lay water supply to Reserve Trench. 49th Brigade area changed. Brigade front from POSEN ALLEY to CAMERON ALLEY. R.E. Store at QUARRY DUMP moved to new Dump near SOUTHERN SAP. Work as on 8.8.16. except that our area to South was taken over from No4 Division & old area N. of POSEN ALLEY was handed over to 155th Field Coy R.E.	
	10.8.16		Work as on 9.8.16	
	11.8.16		Work as on 10.8.16	
	12.8.16		Work as on 11.8.16. Bn Relief in 14 Bis Section	
	13.8.16		Work as on 12.8.16.	
	14.8.16		Work as on 13.8.16. Lt Leahy detailed as officer in charge of repairs to billets. Geo ... was to have been let off but was unfavourable. 12 R.E. from No 4 section sent to assist Geo Coy	
	15.8.16		Work as on 14.8.16. No 1 section relieved No 4 in Xth AVENUE. 12 R.E. from No 4 Section detailed to assist Geo Coy. Wires of own informants. Lt Black & 4 of No 4 Sector proceeded to VERQUIN for Geo course.	

WAR DIARY 157th Field Coy R.E.

or INTELLIGENCE SUMMARY

Army Form C. 2118

(Erase heading not required.)

Place	Date	Hour	Summary of Events and Information	Remarks and references to Appendices
PHILOSOPHE	16.8.16		12 Men detailed as usual for Special Gas Coy. Weather unfavourable.	
	17.8.16		Work as on 15.8.16. Battalion relief in 14 Bis Section	
			Work as on 16.8.16	
			12 Men detailed to assist Special Gas Coy. Weather again unfavourable	
	18.8.16		Work as on 17.8.16	
	19.8.16		Work as on 18.8.16	
	20.8.16		Work as on 19.8.16. Battalion relief in 14 Bis Section	
		10.30 pm	Gas discharged in 14 Bis Section N of the CHALK PIT & in HULLUCH Section.	
			12 Sappers assisted Special RE Gas Coy	
	21.8.16		Work as on 20.8.16	
	22.8.16		Work as on 21.8.16	
			Court of Inquiry held on injuries sustained by Driver Harris	
			No 3 Section relieved No 2 Section in X Avenue.	
	23.8.16	1.30 pm	Message received from C.R.E. to the effect that the company would move to billets in RUITZ on 24.8.16.	
			Nos 1 & 3 Section recalled from X Avenue, all work stopped, Pontoon waggons not loaded.	
		9.20 pm	Orders received from C.R.E. as to route and hour of starting	
	24.8.16	10 AM	Company started for RUITZ	
RUITZ		1.30	Company arrived at RUITZ & went into billets.	

WAR DIARY
or
INTELLIGENCE SUMMARY

(Erase heading not required.)

Army Form C. 2118

157 Field Coy R.E

Place	Date	Hour	Summary of Events and Information	Remarks and references to Appendices
RUITZ	24.8.16	5.30pm	Visited by C.R.E. with orders to move to MARLE LES MINES on 25.8.16.	
	25.8.16	7.0am	Company left for MARLES LES MINES	
MARLE S LES MINES	25.8.16	9.15am	Company arrived & went into billets	
	26.8.16	6.0am	Received orders re entraining. Times to be issued later. (From CRE)	
	27.8.16	1.30am	Received further orders re entraining from 49th Inf Bde. Times to be issued later	
		3.30pm	Received orders to entrain at FOUQUEREUIL at 6.30 pm on 29.8.16	
		5.30pm	Men had baths	
	28.8.16		Company drilled in Sections under Section Officers	
		2.45pm	Visited by C.R.E.	
	29.8.16	8.0am	Received orders as to new billeting areas. SAILLY LE SEC, or VAUX SUR SOMME.	
	29.8.16	6.10pm	Entrained & left FOUQUEREUIL. 3 Sappers arrived as reinforcements	
LONGEAU	30.8.16	4.15am	Arrived, & marched to new billeting area	
SAILLY LE SEC		11.30am	Arrived in new billeting area.	
		12.40pm	Received orders to move at 7.0 am on 31-8-16	
	31.8.16	7.0am	Left SAILLY LE SEC	
HAPPY VALLEY CAMP		11.0am	Arrived & settled down into tents & bivouacs. Situated in 49th Inf. Bde Group.	

Murray
Capt RE
O.C. 157 Fd Coy RE

WAR DIARY

157th Field Company R.E.

FOR MONTH OF SEPTEMBER, 1916.

VOLUME 10

WAR DIARY

157th Field Coy R.E.   Army Form C. 2118

INTELLIGENCE SUMMARY

(Erase heading not required.)

Instructions regarding War Diaries and Intelligence Summaries are contained in F.S. Regs., Part II. and the Staff Manual respectively. Title Pages will be prepared in manuscript.

Place	Date	Hour	Summary of Events and Information	Remarks and references to Appendices
HAPPY VALLEY	1.9.16		Company in Camp in 49th Infy Bde group	
—"—	2.9.16	9.40am	Orders received to be ready to move at 4 hrs notice from B.O. cx on 2.9.16	
—"—	2.9.16	6.15 pm	Orders received for Coy to move to CITADEL at 9.30 am on 3.9.16	
—"—	3.9.16	9.30 am	Coy left.	
CITADEL	—"—	10.45 am	Coy arrived & moved into Camp & bivouac	
—"—	—"—	8.0 pm	Message from CRE to say that in event of 49th Infy Bde moving, the R.E. would remain & come under orders of the Division.	
—"—	—"—	8.30 pm	49th Infy Bde left CITADEL.	
—"—	4.9.16	10.0 am	Orders received to shift camp across the valley	
—"—	5.9.16		Company moved to Bivouac at BILLON Farm	
BRIQUETERIE	6.9.16		Company moved to BRIQUETERIE for work under 49th Infy Bde. Worked in conjunction with a Coy of Hants Pioneers on laying out a track for rails and carts towards ARROW HEAD COPSE. 1 a Cpl wounded.	
—"—	7.9.16	5.0 pm	Orders to move to GUILLEMONT received	
—"—	7.9.16	6.0 pm	left BRIQUETERIE	
GUILLEMONT	7.9.16	6.0 pm	Arrived. After much delay found Commandant & received orders to take over trenches of GUILLEMONT defences from "IRISH RIFLES". Very difficult to obtain trenches owing to dark night & found them a mass of shell holes. Relief partly completed at dawn. 2 coys of HANTS. 155, 156 & 157 Field Coys forming garrison. 48th Bde & 217th Bde in the line in front. 48th Bde left 417 on right. 157 Field coy at disposal of 47 & 7 Bde.	
—"—	8.9.16	3.0 am	Reinforcements received from 47 Infy Bde for work on right 7/8th. Too late to get to work	

WAR DIARY 157th Field Coy R.E.
INTELLIGENCE SUMMARY
(Erase heading not required.)

Army Form C. 2118

Place	Date	Hour	Summary of Events and Information	Remarks and references to Appendices
GUILLEMONT	8.9.16	7.0 a.m	Received verbal instructions from 47th In/ Bde as to work on night 8/9th. Arranged with O.C. Batts (Royal Irish and Munsters) as to details of work during the evening.	
—	—	10 p.m	Received orders from C.R.E. to move to BERNAFAY WOOD on being relieved by 49th In/ 8th during night of 8th/9th.	
—	—	3.0 p.m	Message received cancelling above. 157th Field Coy to remain with 47th In/ Bde for work. During the night Nos 2, 3, 9 & 4 Sections worked with the 8th Munsters, 6th Royal Irish and 7th Leinsters in preparing new trenches for attacking purpose.	
—	—		Orders received to the effect that the 16th Division would attack GUINCHY on 9.9.16. That 157th Field Coy R.E. would be required to assist the 6th Connaughts and 8th Munsters in consolidating two Strong Points behind the new positions when captured. During the afternoon arrangements were made with 6th Connaughts and 8th Munsters as to work for the attack, & the following agreed on:— One half of No 1 Section to report to 6th Connaughts & the other half 8th Munsters before daylight on 9.9.16. These with working parties of Infantry would advance when the attack had reached its final objective and start work on the consolidation of the Strong Points. Nos 3 & 4 Sections would relieve the two half sections at dusk. No 2 Section to remain in reserve & provide runners for inter communication.	
	8.9.16		Casualties 5 Suffers wounded	

WAR DIARY 157th Field Coy RE

Army Form C. 2118

INTELLIGENCE SUMMARY

(Erase heading not required.)

Instructions regarding War Diaries and Intelligence Summaries are contained in F.S. Regs., Part II. and Staff Manual respectively. Title Pages will be prepared in manuscript.

Place	Date	Hour	Summary of Events and Information	Remarks and references to Appendices
GUILLEMONT	9.9.16		During early hours of morning received message that attack would not take place until 4.45 p.m., so did not send No.1 Section to trenches before daylight. The 5 section for 6th Connaughts went about 10 a.m. and the 2 section for the 8th Munsters at 2.30 p.m.	
		4.45	General attack by 16th Division. The attack did not reach its final objects so no work on the strong points was possible, and No.1 Section was withdrawn before midnight. Nos 3 & 4 did not leave Coy H.Q.	
	10.9.16	40p??/2.30am	Orders received from CRE for Coy to return to MINDEN POST at daylight. Casualties 2 Suffs relieved, 3 Wounded	
		3.15am	4 Grenadier Guards arrived to take our trench occupied by 157th Fd Coy	
			Coy left for MINDEN POST	
MINDEN POST		8.0am	Coy arrived, & received orders to hand over work to 71st Field Coy RE & proceed MORLANCOURT at 2.0 p.m.	
		2.0pm	Coy left for MORLANCOURT	
		5.30pm	Coy arrived & went into billets. Casualties 3 suffs wounded.	
MORLANCOURT	11.9.16	10.0am	Orders received to move with 49th M/GUN Group to SAILLY LE SEC at 6.0pm	

Army Form C. 2118

WAR DIARY
or
INTELLIGENCE SUMMARY
(Erase heading not required.)

157/5 Fld Coy. R.E.

Instructions regarding War Diaries and Intelligence Summaries are contained in F. S. Regs., Part II. and Staff Manual respectively. Title Pages will be prepared in manuscript.

Place	Date	Hour	Summary of Events and Information	Remarks and references to Appendices
MORLANCOURT	11.9.16	9.0 p.m.	Coy. joined 49th Bde. & proceeded to SAILLY LE SEC.	
SAILLY LE SEC	" "	9.0 p.m.	Coy. arrived & went into billets	
	12.9.16	4.0 p.m.	visited by C.R.E.	
	13.9.16		General Company training.	
	14.9.16		Work as on 13th	
	15.9.16		Work as on 14th	
	" "	5 p.m.	O.C. went to hospital	
	16.9.16		Work as on 15th	
	" "	11.30 p.m.	Received message from C.R.E. stating that 16th Division was to be relieved. Transport & mounted personnel starting afternoon 17th, to move as follows:— Transport & dismounts by bus 18th. infantry & dismounts by bus 18th.	
	17.9.16	10.a.m.	Church Parade for dismounted men.	
	" "	2 p.m.	Transport & mounted personnel of Coy. left SAILLY LE SEC with remainder of 49th Bde. Transport & proceeded to LA CHAUSSEE via LA NEUVILLE, DAOURS	
LA CHAUSSEE	18.9.16	12.30 a.m.	Transport etc. arrived at LA CHAUSSEE & went into billets	
	" "	10.15 a.m.	Transport etc. left LA CHAUSSEE & proceeded to FRESNELLE & AMIENS.	

Army Form C. 2118

WAR DIARY
or
INTELLIGENCE SUMMARY
(Erase heading not required.)

157th Fld Coy R.E.

Place	Date	Hour	Summary of Events and Information	Remarks and references to Appendices
SAILLY LE SEC	18/9/16	10:15 a.m.	Dismounted portion of Company left SAILLY LE SEC with 49th Bde. Group (Divn Ft) & marched to LA NEUVILLE	
LA NEUVILLE	"	12:30 p.m.	49th Bde. Group reaches LA NEUVILLE – VECQUEMONT Rd where French motor lorries were lined up. Remainder of 16th Division was also waiting on this road.	
"	"	2:0 p.m.	Buses left with Company & with Remainder of ERONDELLE transport arrived & halted at ERONDELLE	
ERONDELLE	"	5:30 p.m.	Officers & 2 two-bus of Company (abt ½ coy) arrived within 1 mile of ERONDELLE	
ERONDELLE	"	8:0 p.m.	½ coy. reached ERONDELLE, marching from bus terminus.	
"	"	8:30 p.m.		
"	"	9:45 p.m.	Other ½ coy (divn Ft) arrived at ERONDELLE. There men were delayed on road owing to two breakdowns.	
"	"	10:0 p.m.	Whole company settled down in billets.	
"	19.9.16	3:30 p.m.	visited by G.O.C. 49th/Bde. & informed by him that division would entrain on 21.9.16.	
"	"	4:0 p.m.	reinforcements arrived. Received preliminary entraining orders.	
"	20.9.16	1:0 a.m.	General Company training. Received final entraining orders, details of refilling etc.	

WAR DIARY 157th Field Coy. R.E.
or
INTELLIGENCE SUMMARY
(Erase heading not required.)

Army Form C. 2118

Place	Date	Hour	Summary of Events and Information	Remarks and references to Appendices
ERQUINGHEM	20.9.16	5.0 p.m	8 reinforcements arrived.	
"	21.9.16	9.0 a.m	Coy. left for PONT REMY station.	
PONT REMY	"	10.0 A.M	Coy. arrived & entrained.	
"	"	1.8 p.m.	Train left with coy. (Orders re billeting received en route)	
BAILLEUL	"	10.0 p.m.	Coy. arrived at BAILLEUL & detrained	
"	22.9.16	10 A.M.	Coy. left for KEMMEL leaving transport at SCHERPENBERG (M.12.c.7.1.)	
KEMMEL	"	4.0 A.M	Coy. arrived at billeting area (N.15.c.0.6) near KEMMEL	
"	"	2.0 p.m	Check Parade. Coy. worked on billets.	
"	23.9.16	7.30 p.m	Interviewed O.C. Canadian Fd. Coy. which we were going to relieve.	
"	"		Took over work, maps, stores etc.	
"	23.9.16	9.0 A.M.	Section officers went round the line with officers of Canadian R.E.	
"	"		Men worked on improving billets etc.	
"	24.9.16	1.0 a.m	Divisional relief took place. (16th relieves 4th Canadian Div.) Orders received from C.R.E. that 1 Section was to be employed on control & maintenance of tramway system. The Officer i/charge was to report to R.T.O. 4th Canadian Division at 7 a.m.	

WAR DIARY
or
INTELLIGENCE SUMMARY
(Erase heading not required.)

Army Form C. 2118

Place	Date	Hour	Summary of Events and Information	Remarks and references to Appendices
KEMMEL	24.9.16	7.0 a.m.	Officer details from tramway work reported to R.T.O. & took over from him.	
"	"	9.0 a.m.	Section left billets to work in 49th Bgd. Area (Rylt-Bgr. front)	
"	"		Orders received that field Companies would work under brigades.	
"	"	10.0 a.m.	Went round the line & reported to O.C. left & right battalions.	
"	"	3.0 p.m.	Returned to Billets.	
"	"	3.45 p.m.	Reported to Bgd. Hd. Qrs.	
"	"		G.O.C. Bgr. suggested improvement to road like made in right section.	
"	"	7.0 p.m.	Visited C.R.E.	
"	25.9.16	8 a.m.	Sections left billets for work. Work carried out as agreed upon by G.O.C. 49th F./52r.	
"	"		Work of Coy. anenfys as follows:—	
"	"		Revetting general improvement in front line arrivals by infantry.	
"	"		No 1 Section	
"	"		No 2 Section Tramway control & maintenance.	
"	"		No 3 Section Drainage work in right section	
"	"		No 4 Section Revetting of Spar MARR.	

WAR DIARY or INTELLIGENCE SUMMARY

Army Form C. 2118

157th Field Coy R.E.

Place	Date	Hour	Summary of Events and Information	Remarks and references to Appendices
KEMMEL	25.9.16	11 a.m.	Attended conference of Coy. Commanders presided over by C.R.E. The following points were discussed & settled:- Allotting of Wrk. to 2 field Companies in the line. Management of R.E. Stores & Ramways. Management of field company reliefs. Arrangement by Brigade headquarters, & army as with Brigadiers &c. Reported at Brigade headquarters, 8 hours a day. work appears to be unusual occurrence.	
"	26.9.16		Work carried on.	
"	27.9.16		Work carried on.	
		4 p.m.	Capt. P.T. Whittall arrived and assumed Command of the Company.	
"	28.9.16		Distribution of work as follows:- No.1 Section Lieu. J.S. Mren. work in Right subsector with 8th R.I.F. No.2 Section Trench Railway maintenance & construction. 2 Lt. McHaffie acting as R.T.O. No.3 Section Lieu. Coo 7 men working on drainage of Brigade Trench area.	

WAR DIARY
or
INTELLIGENCE SUMMARY
(Erase heading not required.)

157th Field Coy. R.E.

Army Form C. 2118

Place	Date	Hour	Summary of Events and Information	Remarks and references to Appendices
KEMMEL	28/9/16 contd.		No. 4 Section working on Pall Mall C.T. 2/Lt. Leahy with 7 men No. 1 and 7 men No. 3 working with 7th R.I.F. in left sub-section. Work by parts of 3 men from each section started on Officers' billets.	
		4 pm.	Visited B.G.C. 49th I.B. to talk over work.	
		5.30 pm.	Visited O.C. 7th R.I.F. to discuss work.	
KEMMEL	29/9/16	9.30 am.	Made round of trenches with O.C. 7th R.I.F. by appointment. Chose site for new Company Headquarters. Work continued as detailed for 28th. General condition of trenches fair, but much work required if they are to stand under heavy rain. Reserve line wants putting in order. 2/Lt. Black 91 h.Coy attended Gas lecture.	
	30/9/16		Work continued as above.	

P. A. Nuttall
Capt., R.E.
O.C. 157th (Field) Coy. R.E.

WAR DIARY

MONTH OF OCTOBER, 1916.

VOLUME No. 11

157th Field Co. R.E.

WAR DIARY
INTELLIGENCE SUMMARY

Army Form C. 2118

157th Field Coy. R.E.

October 1916

Place	Date	Hour	Summary of Events and Information	Remarks and references to Appendices
KEMMEL	1/10/16		Work organised as previously – i.e. No.1 Section work in Right Sub-sector (leaves 7 men) No.2 " " " on Railways in Divisional area. " 3 " " " on Drainage of Brigade Area (49th I.B) (leaves 7 men) " 4 " " " on PALL-MALL C.T. 2/Lt Leahy and 14 men from No.1 & 3 Sections work in left subsector. Capt. E.K. Greenhow goes to hospital.	
	2/10/16		Make tour of trenches visiting YOUNG St. & Reserve line to inspect work there. Lt. Bolton proceeded to join C.R.E. for shutting work. No. 3 Sec. Taken over by 2/Lt Leahy. Work as usual. Visited C.R.E. to confer with him re supply of certain stores. 3 men of each section working on Officers' Billets which are so far non-existent.	
	3/10/16	7.45 pm	"Wind Safe" message received. Today 75% of Coy. went through for baths Chaubers in new Box Respirators. Remainder of Coy went thro' Gas test.	
	4/10/16		Visited Trenches, found Billet VIGO St., PICCADILLY, front-line, PALL MALL &c. with O.C. 7th Innerskilling Fusiliers & O.C. 49th Bde. discussing new Coy's H.Q.	

Army Form C. 2118

WAR DIARY
or
INTELLIGENCE SUMMARY
(Erase heading not required.)

157th Field Coy. R.E.

Place	Date	Hour	Summary of Events and Information	Remarks and references to Appendices
KEMMEL	5/10/16	7 am	All Coy do ½ hours work sandbagging billets.	
		8.30 am	Usual work continued. Sample dugout made as pattern for manufacture in Divisional shops, many being required still in this area.	
	6/10/16		Work as before.	
	7/10/16		Work as usual.	
	8/10/16		Work as usual. Visited left subsector & finally chose new Coy HQ in KETCHEN AVENUE, & inspected other work there.	
	9/10/16		Work as usual.	
	10/10/16		Work as usual. Capt Greenhow rejoined from Hospital. Visited trenches with G.S.O.1. & B.M. 49th I.B., explaining work.	
	11/10/16		The new L.R.E. held conference of Field Coy Commanders, settling various points re "reliefs" &c. No. 3 Section left as permanent hutting party under C.R.E., all other details being sent to rejoin Company. Visited Bde. H.Q. & interviewed General on reorganisation of work.	

Army Form C. 2118

WAR DIARY
INTELLIGENCE SUMMARY 157 2d Fd Coy R.E.
(Erase heading not required.)

Place	Date	Hour	Summary of Events and Information	Remarks and references to Appendices
REMMEL	12/10/16		No 2 Section partially relieved from Railway work. Organisation of work now:- No 1 Section (1 NCO 5 men) Right sub-sector L. Humphries. " 2 " " " 12 men on Tramway construction L. Ratcliffe. " 3 " " " Away shutting under CRE " 4 " " " (less 5 men) Left sub-sector 2/L. Black. (less 5 men) Lieut. Bird with 5 men each of No. 1 & 4 Sections & 10 men of No 2 to carry on & finish PALL MALL. In addition to above 4 NCOs & 9 men are working with 1 N.C.O. & 8 men of Infantry each on Reserve trench. Progress is good.	
	13/10/16		Work as usual.	
	14/10/16		Work as usual. Enemy by an usual exhibition of liveliness stopped most of the work in left subsector by a certain amount of shelling. 20 Infantry have now practically relieved No 2 Section of all railway work except a small party on construction. Many new Dugouts are required as the Brigade luggy to be strengthened. At a Conference with 13 G.C. 4.13 m Today form of work to be started tomorrow was approved. Capt. & H. Greenhow proceeds on leave.	

Army Form C. 2118

WAR DIARY
INTELLIGENCE SUMMARY
(Erase heading not required.)

157ᵗʰ Field Coy. R. E.

Instructions regarding War Diaries and Intelligence Summaries are contained in F.S. Regs., Part II. and the Staff Manual respectively. Title Pages will be prepared in manuscript.

Place	Date	Hour	Summary of Events and Information	Remarks and references to Appendices
KEMMEL	15/10/16		Sites chosen for 10 new Dugouts at YONGE ST. DUGOUTS. Material for frames, railway sent up by night & excavations begun. Re-Organization now :- No 1. (less 5 men) Right Subsector. No 2. (less 10 men) Railways No 3. Hutting No 4. (less 5 men 9 Officers) Pall Mall, + drainage thereof. ½: Black & 20 men Left Subsector.	
	16/10/16		Work as above. —	
	17/10/16		Work as before. — 9 Dugouts at YONGE ST completed for shelter of Stronger Coy. which came in today.	
	18/10/16		Conference with O.C. 2ⁿᵈ Royal Irish Regt. re work to be undertaken. Other work continued as usual.	
	19/10/16		Pall Mall badly damaged during night — repairs undertaken. 8 parties of 1 NCO & 8 men started in front line — Left Subsector each with 1 Sapper.	

Army Form C. 2118

WAR DIARY
INTELLIGENCE SUMMARY
(Erase heading not required.)

157th Field Coy. R.E.

Place	Date	Hour	Summary of Events and Information	Remarks and references to Appendices
KEMMEL	20/10/16		Work as usual. New road thro' Kemmel Chateau grounds surveyed & report made (posted). Sharpe front in morning.	
	21/10/16		Work as before. Framing &c. of floors in part of Pall Mall finished, new work continued. Frosty weather.	
	22/10/16		Work as usual. New parties put on to LINDENHOEK Road Tramline to put in good state of repair for Mule Haulage. Strengthening of Brewery in Kemmel for Dressing Station arranged. Frosty & clear.	
	23/10/16		Construction of emplacements for Stokes Guns commenced, also survey of trenches. Two experimental dug-outs in Reserve Trench completed. O.C. inspected route for proposed road thro' KEMMEL Chateau grounds. Other work as usual, except that it is very difficult to make certain that Infantry parties on front line work with our assistance will be available for regular hours. Weather changes - much warmer. No.1 relieved No.3 Sec. at Stuttung.	
	24/10/16	11:40 am 11:55	Work continued as before. A damp wet day which always slows up the work. No. 3 Section started work in Right Sub sector. Test Gas Alarm received.	

WAR DIARY

Army Form C. 2118

15th 7th Field Coy. R.E.

Place	Date	Hour	Summary of Events and Information	Remarks and references to Appendices
KEMMEL	25/10/16		Work as usual.	
	26/10/16		Work as before.	
	27/10/16		Work as usual.	
	28/10/16		Work as usual. Considerable damage done to our front line by Enemy Trench Mortars.	
	29/10/16	10 a.m.	Lecture by O.C. Coy. on Various subjects affecting discipline & sanitation. Inspection of Boxrespirators, Iron Rations, Field Dressings & Gas Drill.	
		5.45pm	Raiding party with two detonators (M.B.) & fuzes attached ready to insert in charge went over to German lines after Artillery preparation. The party on right got hung up in wire – the left party got into Enemy's trenches and before leaving demolished a machine gun emplacement. Our trenches were further damaged by enemy retaliation.	
	30/10/16		Work as usual. A very wet day.	

WAR DIARY
or
INTELLIGENCE SUMMARY 157th Field Coy. R.E.

(Erase heading not required.)

Army Form C. 2118

Place	Date	Hour	Summary of Events and Information	Remarks and references to Appendices
KEMMEL	31/10/16		Work as usual. Fairly fine day. – Showery.	

P.F. Whittall
Capt., R.E.
O.C. 157th (Field) Coy. R.E.

WAR DIARY.

FOR

MONTH OF NOVEMBER, 1916.

VOLUME 12

157th Field Coy. R.E.

WAR DIARY
INTELLIGENCE SUMMARY

157th Field Coy. R.E.

Army Form C. 2118

Place	Date	Hour	Summary of Events and Information	Remarks and references to Appendices
KEMMEL	1/11/16		Congratulations of Army Commander received on work accomplished in raid on 29th ulto. Distribution: No. 1 Section Hutting. " 2 Pall Mall & Back Area. " 3 Right Subsector. " 4 Left " .	
	2/11/16		Work as usual.	
	3/11/16		1 O.R. wounded (at duty) (Sap. Phillips)	
	4/11/16		Rust stopped at 2 p.m. for operations. 3 O.R. reinforcements arrived.	
	5/11/16		—	
	6/11/16		Usual weekly inspection & lecture by Lt. Snowdon on Explosives & testing an Exploder. No. 4 Section relieved No. 1 on Hutting.	

WAR DIARY or INTELLIGENCE SUMMARY

Army Form C. 2118

(Erase heading not required.)

Place	Date	Hour	Summary of Events and Information	Remarks and references to Appendices
KEMMEL	7/11/16		Distribution of Work. No. 1 Left Subsector.	
			" 2. Tramways, Pall Mall &c.	
			" 3. Right Subsector	
			" 4. Hutting.	
	8/11/16		Work as usual. a/Cpl. McAllen passed as Shoeing Smith by Board.	
	9/11/16			
	10/11/16			
	11/11/16			
	12/11/16			
	13/11/16		Usual weekly inspection. Lecture by Lt. McHaffie on field service Regulations. Capt. P. Nuttall proceeded to WIMEREUX for instruction in Camouflage.	

WAR DIARY
or
INTELLIGENCE SUMMARY

Army Form C. 2118

Instructions regarding War Diaries and Intelligence Summaries are contained in F. S. Regs., Part II. and Staff Manual respectively. Title Pages will be prepared in manuscript.

(*Erase heading not required.*)

Place	Date	Hour	Summary of Events and Information	Remarks and references to Appendices
KEMMEL	14/10/16		Work as usual - 3 reinforcements arrived.	
	15/10/16			
	16/10/16		Capt. P.L. Whittall rejoined from WIMEREUX.	
	17/10/16		2/Lt. M. J.W. McGaffie admitted to Hospital	
	18/10/16			
	19/10/16		Monthly periodical inspection. Lecture by O.C. Coy. on organisation of a Field Coy.	
	20/10/16		Work as usual.	
	21/10/16			
	22/10/16		Special 2" T.M. & Stokes Gun emplacements commenced, with assistance from other Field Coys. Drawings provided for Pioneers to work to.	

1875 Wt. W593/826 1,000,000 4/15 J.B.C. & A. A.D.S.S./Forms/C.2118.

Army Form C. 2118

WAR DIARY
or
INTELLIGENCE SUMMARY
(Erase heading not required.)

Instructions regarding War Diaries and Intelligence Summaries are contained in F. S. Regs., Part II. and Staff Manual respectively. Title Pages will be prepared in manuscript.

Place	Date	Hour	Summary of Events and Information	Remarks and references to Appendices
KEMMEL	23/4/16		Work as usual.	
	24/4/16		Usual periodical inspection. Lecture by O.C. Coy on Camouflage.	
	25/4/16		Work as usual.	
	26/4/16		————	
	27/4/16		2 Emplacements sent up for Stokes guns — but not erected as carrying parties failed to obtain work. 2 Sappers transferred to 158 Coy.	
	28/4/16		Work as before. 2 emplacements sent up & reached destination. 2 Lt. G. H. B. oster joined coy as reinforcement. 1 Sapper wounded (Johnson)	
	29/4/16		Work as usual.	

Army Form C. 2118

WAR DIARY
or
INTELLIGENCE SUMMARY
(Erase heading not required.)

Instructions regarding War Diaries and Intelligence Summaries are contained in F. S. Regs., Part II. and Staff Manual respectively. Title Pages will be prepared in manuscript.

Place	Date	Hour	Summary of Events and Information	Remarks and references to Appendices
KEMMEL	30th /4/16		had periodical inspection. Parade service at noon. Lt. Leahy took over No. 2. Section & relieved No. 4 section at Shutting.	

P. A. Nuttall
Capt., R.E.
O.C. 157th (Field) Coy. R.E.

WAR DIARY FOR MONTH OF DECEMBER, 1916.

VOLUME 13.

157th Field Coy. R.E.

WAR DIARY or INTELLIGENCE SUMMARY

Army Form C. 2118

Place	Date	Hour	Summary of Events and Information	Remarks and references to Appendices
KEMMEL	1/12/16		Orders received that Company were to take over part of sector held by 36th Division. Distribution of Work :- No 1 Left Sub. sector; " 2 Nutting; " 3 Pall Mall and Back Area; " 4 Right Sub-sector.	
	2/12/16		Work as usual. Above order cancelled. False gas alarm received 9.45 p.m.	
	3/12/16		Work as usual. Lieut. Monckton went on leave (4th to 14th). Lieut. Bolton rejoined Company.	
	4/12/16		Work as usual. Intimation received that Capt. Granshaw granted month's sick leave from 25/11/16 by Standing Medical Board.	
	5/12/16		Work as usual. Sub-sector extended 400 ft to left by inclusion of part of line taken over from 48th Brigade. Reconnoitred Hill 74 with Lieut. Kenrick of Special Works Park.	

WAR DIARY
or
INTELLIGENCE SUMMARY
(Erase heading not required.)

Army Form C. 2118

Place	Date	Hour	Summary of Events and Information	Remarks and references to Appendices
KEMMEL	6/12/16		Work as usual. O.C. went on leave (9th to 17th); Lieut. Bolton taking temporary command. Intimation received that Capt. Greenhow passed unfit for general service and struck off strength from 14/10/16.	
	7/12/16		Usual weekly inspection. Lecture by 2/Lieut. Black on "Uses of Engineers in the Field."	
	8/12/16		Reconnoitred line for new communication trench. Work as usual.	
	9/12/16		Work as usual. Conference with C.R.E. re new communication trench, and with Brigade Major re T.M. emplacements.	
	10/12/16		Work as usual. Orders received that all ordinary work to be stopped and whole Coy. (less Hutting section) to concentrate on T.M. emplacements.	
	11/12/16		Whole Coy. (less section on Hutting) working on T.M. emplacements. Reconnoitred site for dressing station at LINDENHOEK.	
	12/12/16		Work as on 11th.	

WAR DIARY
or
INTELLIGENCE SUMMARY

Army Form C. 2118

Place	Date	Hour	Summary of Events and Information	Remarks and references to Appendices
KEMMEL	13/12/16		Usual inspection. One reinforcement (sapper) arrived. Intimation received that Lieut. Monckton to report for permanent duty on transfer to 136th Army Troops Co.	
	14/12/16		Work as usual. Accompanied O.R.E. round line.	
	15/12/16		Work as usual.	
	16/12/16		" " "	
	17/12/16		" " "	
	18/12/16		Usual inspection. O.b. returned from leave.	
	19/12/16		Work as usual.	
	20/12/16		" " " One reinforcement (sapper) arrived. Reconnoitred line with Lieut. Kerwick of Special Works Park. Lieut. Monckton reported as "About" without leave. "Thistle periscope erected on Hill 74.	

Army Form C. 2118

WAR DIARY
or
INTELLIGENCE SUMMARY
(Erase heading not required.)

Instructions regarding War Diaries and Intelligence Summaries are contained in F.S. Regs., Part II. and the Staff Manual respectively. Title Pages will be prepared in manuscript.

Place	Date	Hour	Summary of Events and Information	Remarks and references to Appendices
KEMMEL	21/12/15		Work as usual. Parapet O.P. nearly north of GLORY HOLE.	
	22/12/15		" " "	
	23/12/15		" " "	
	24/12/15		" " Reconnoitred site for Battle O.P. at GOETHAL'S FARM.	
	25/12/15		General Church Parade. Divisional Commander visited L.R.B. Camp and addressed the Company.	
	26/12/15		Work as usual.	
	27/12/15		" " "	
	28/12/15		" " " 2/Lieut. Healy admitted to hospital.	

WAR DIARY
or
INTELLIGENCE SUMMARY

Army Form C. 2118

Place	Date	Hour	Summary of Events and Information	Remarks and references to Appendices
KEMMEL	29/12/16		No 3 section relieved No 2 section on truthing. Distribution of Work:- No 1 section - Left Sub-sector; " 2 " - Pall Mall and Back Area; " 3 " - Truthing; " 4 " - Right Sub-sector.	
	30/12/16		Usual inspection. - Lecture by Medical Officer.	
	31/12/16		Work as usual.	

J. F. Whittall
Maj. **R.E.**
O.C. 157th (Field) Coy. R.E.

WAR DIARY for month of JANUARY, 1917.

VOLUME 14

Royal Engineers 154th Field Company

Army Form C. 2118.

15th Field Company R.E.

WAR DIARY
INTELLIGENCE SUMMARY.
January 1917.

Place	Date	Hour	Summary of Events and Information	Remarks and references to Appendices
KEMMEL	1/1/17.		Distribution of Work :- No.1 sector - Left sub-sector;	
			" 2 " - Pall Mall and Back Area;	
			" 3 " - Hutting;	
			" 4 " - Right sub-sector.	
	2/1/17.		Work as usual.	
	3/1/17.		" " "	
	4/1/17.		" " "	
	5/1/17.		Rest day. Usual periodical inspections and Church parade.	
	6/1/17.		Work as usual. 2 reinforcements (Drivers) arrived.	
	7/1/17.		" " " Wind "dangerous."	

WAR DIARY

~~INTELLIGENCE~~ SUMMARY.

(Erase heading not required.)

Army Form C. 2118.

157th Field Company R.E.
January 1917.

Place	Date	Hour	Summary of Events and Information	Remarks and references to Appendices
KEMMEL	8/1/17		Work as usual. Accompanied C.R.E. round line and reconnoitred new support line and communication trenches. Wind "safe."	
	9/1/17		Work as usual. Wind "dangerous."	
	10/1/17		" — " — " . G.O.C. visited Camp.	
	11/1/17		Rest day. — Usual periodical inspections and lecture by O.C. — 1 W.O. transferred to Advanced Horse Transport Depot. Wind "safe."	
	12/1/17	4.10 p.m.	In left sub-sector all ordinary work stopped to reclaim VIA GELIA and KETCHEN AVENUE as far as possible where destroyed by enemy's fire. — 2/Lieut. Lealy returned from hospital. — Weather very wet and stormy.	

WAR DIARY

~~INTELLIGENCE SUMMARY~~
(Erase heading not required.)

Army Form C. 2118.

157th Field Company, R.E.
January 1917.

Instructions regarding War Diaries and Intelligence Summaries are contained in F. S. Regs., Part II. and the Staff Manual respectively. Title pages will be prepared in manuscript.

Place	Date	Hour	Summary of Events and Information	Remarks and references to Appendices
KEMMEL	13/1/17		Work as usual. – 2/Lieut. Leahy went on leave (14th – 24th). – Casualty – 1 sapper killed. Weather – same as yesterday.	
	14/1/17		" – " – " – On visiting trenches, discovered junction of PALL MALL and front line badly knocked about; front line wiped out in 2 places, each between 20 and 30 yards. Special arrangements made for re-making. – Capt. E. K. Kynaston rejoined Company. – 2/Lieut. E. O'D. Burke-Gaffney joined Company on transfer from 57th Field Company R.E. – Weather – dry and frosty.	
	15/1/17		Work as usual. Weather – very wet and cold.	
		5.20 p.	Wind "dangerous."	
	16/1/17		Work as usual. – Intimation received that Lieut. F. H. Monckton struck off strength of Company from 4/12/16. – Weather – heavy fall of snow.	

Army Form C. 2118.

WAR DIARY

154th Field Company R.E.

INTELLIGENCE SUMMARY.

January 1917.

(Erase heading not required.)

Instructions regarding War Diaries and Intelligence Summaries are contained in F.S. Regs, Part II. and the Staff Manual respectively. Title pages will be prepared in manuscript.

Place	Date	Hour	Summary of Events and Information	Remarks and references to Appendices
KEMMEL	14/1/17		Rest day. - Usual inspections and Church parade. - Accompanied C.R.E. round line. Weather - same as yesterday.	
	18/1/17	9.45am.	Work as usual. - 1 reinforcement (sapper) arrived. - Weather - slight fall of snow. Wind "safe".	
	19/1/17		Work as usual. - Daily party of 40 from Entrenching Battalion commenced - put on to work at REGENTS DUGOUTS. - Weather - dry and cold; hard frost.	
	20/1/17	6am.	Work as usual. - Weather - same as yesterday. Wind "dangerous."	
	21/1/17		Work as usual. - Ceremonial parade at DE ZON for presentation by C.R.E. of Divisional Parchment Certificates. - Weather - same as yesterday.	

WAR DIARY

151th Field Company R.E.

Army Form C. 2118.

INTELLIGENCE SUMMARY

January 1917.

(Erase heading not required.)

Place	Date	Hour	Summary of Events and Information	Remarks and references to Appendices
KEMMEL	22/1/17		No 1 section relieved No 3 section on halting, No 3 taking over work in left sub-sector. Zwolle taken of S.P. 10. - Weather - same as yesterday.	
	23/1/17		Rest day. - Usual inspections and lectures by O.C. - Weather - same as yesterday.	
	24/1/17	11 a.m.	No 2 section took over work in right sub-sector. No 4 taking over Back Area. "Lot Stock Broadway." - Weather - same as yesterday.	
	25/1/17		Work as usual. - 2/Lieut. Ferby returned from leave. - 2/Lieut. Black went on leave (26th Jany to 5th Feby.) - Weather - same as yesterday.	
	26/1/17		Work as usual. - Accompanied C.R.E. round line. - Weather - same as yesterday.	
	27/1/17		" — " — " — Meeting with Brigadier-General re re-organisation of line. - Weather - same as yesterday.	

Army Form C. 2118.

WAR DIARY
INTELLIGENCE SUMMARY
(Erase heading not required.)

January 1917.
157th Field Company, R.E.

Instructions regarding War Diaries and Intelligence Summaries are contained in F. S. Regs., Part II. and the Staff Manual respectively. Title pages will be prepared in manuscript.

Place	Date	Hour	Summary of Events and Information	Remarks and references to Appendices
KEMMEL	28/1/17		Work as usual. - Weather same as yesterday.	
	29/1/17		Rest day. - Usual inspection and Church parade. - 47th I.B. relieved 49th I.B. in line. - Weather same as yesterday.	
	30/1/17		Work as usual. Interviewed O/C the Commanders re work - decided to stop all working parties (except OLD FRENCH TRENCH and loading parties) until frost breaks, as it is impossible to make any impression on the ground. R.E. personnel to be concentrated on such work as can be carried on. - Weather - same as yesterday.	
	31/1/17		Work on new line laid down yesterday commenced.	

P. J. Nuttall
MAJOR, R.E.
O.C. 157th (FIELD) COMPANY R.E.

T2134. Wt. W708-776. 500000. 4/15. Sir J. C. & S.

WAR DIARY.

FOR MONTH OF FEBRUARY, 1917.

VOLUME 15

UNIT:- 15/th Field Coy R.E.

Vol 15

WAR DIARY 154th Field Company, R.E.
of
~~INTELLIGENCE~~ SUMMARY. February 1917.

Army Form C. 2118.

Place	Date	Hour	Summary of Events and Information	Remarks and references to Appendices
KEMMEL	1/2/17		Distribution of Work:- No 1 Section - Hutting.	
	"		" 2 " - Right Sub-sector.	
			" 3 " - Left Sub-sector.	
			" 4 " - Pall Mall and back area.	
	"		Major Whitehall proceeded to LE PARCQ to lecture at R.E. School of Instruction (4th Course). Capt. Greenhow taking over command.	
	"		Casualty :- 1 sapper died of wounds in hospital.	
	"		Weather - keen frost.	
	2/2/17		Work as usual. Weather - same as yesterday.	
	3/2/17		" " " " " "	
	4/2/17		" " " " " "	

WAR DIARY 154th Field Company R.E. Army Form C. 2118.

INTELLIGENCE SUMMARY. February 1917.

(Erase heading not required.)

Place	Date	Hour	Summary of Events and Information	Remarks and references to Appendices
KEMMEL	5/2/17		Work as usual. Reconnoitred ground in rear of front line with a view to reporting to C.R.E. on the opening up of old trenches. Weather - keen frost and sunny.	
	6/2/17.		49th Infantry Brigade relieved 147th Infantry Brigade in line. Usual inspections. 2/Lieut. Black returned from leave. Weather - same as yesterday.	
	7/2/17.		Work as usual. Weather - same as yesterday.	
	8/2/17.		" " " " " " "	
	9/2/17.		" " " " " " "	
	10/2/17.		" " " " " " "	

WAR DIARY
INTELLIGENCE SUMMARY

of 154th Field Company, R.E. Army Form C. 2118.

February 1917.

(Erase heading not required.)

Place	Date	Hour	Summary of Events and Information	Remarks and references to Appendices
KEMMEL	11/2/17		No.tt Section relieved No.1 Section on fatigue. No.1 Section taking over work in back area. Weather - slight snow.	
	12/2/17		Work as usual. Major Whithall rejoined Company. 2/Lieut. Leahy proceeded to 16th Divisional School for course. Weather - thaw.	
	13/2/17		Work as usual. 3 reinforcements (Sappers) arrived. Weather - same as yesterday.	
	14/2/17		Relief day. Usual inspections. Weather - clear and frosty.	
	15/2/17		Work as usual. Weather - same as yesterday.	
	16/2/17		" " " " " "	

Army Form C. 2118.

WAR DIARY
of 154th Field Company, R.E.
INTELLIGENCE SUMMARY. February 1917

(Erase heading not required.)

Instructions regarding War Diaries and Intelligence Summaries are contained in F. S. Regs., Part II. and the Staff Manual respectively. Title pages will be prepared in manuscript.

Place	Date	Hour	Summary of Events and Information	Remarks and references to Appendices
KEMMEL	17/2/17		Work as usual. Gas alarm received 9 p.m.; cancelled 9.34 p.m. Weather - slight showers of rain; misty and frost nearly broken.	
	18/2/17		Work as usual. Weather - same as yesterday.	
	19/2/17		47th Infantry Brigade raided German trenches. Commencement of all work postponed in consequence to 12 noon. During the morning a drill parade was held and tool carts checked. Weather - same as yesterday.	
	20/2/17		Work as usual. Weather - same as yesterday.	
	21/2/17		" " " " " "	
	22/2/17		49th Infantry Brigade relieved 47th Infantry Brigade. Usual inspections and lecture by O.C. Weather - wet and misty.	
		10:50 p.m.	"Wind dangerous".	

WAR DIARY
of
INTELLIGENCE SUMMARY. 157th Field Company R.E.

February 1917.

(Erase heading not required.)

Army Form C. 2118.

Place	Date	Hour	Summary of Events and Information	Remarks and references to Appendices
KEMMEL	23/2/17		Work as usual. 1 reinforcement (Sergeant) arrived. Weather - dull but fair.	
"	24/2/17		" " " " . Weather - same as yesterday.	
"		5.15 p.m.	Enemy dropped gas shells in KEMMEL; men of Company warned to have respirators ready as precaution.	
"	25/2/17		No. 3 section relieved No. 4 section on pontoons. No. 4 section taking over work in left sub-sector. 1 N.C.O. proceeded to 16th Divisional School for 4th course of instruction. 1 N.C.O. returning from 3rd course. Weather - same as yesterday.	
"	26/2/17		Work as usual. 2/Lieut. Fealy rejoined from 16th Divisional School. Weather - clear and fine.	
"		10.35 a.m.	Wind "safe".	
"	27/2/17		Work as usual. Weather - same as yesterday.	

WAR DIARY
INTELLIGENCE SUMMARY

Army Form C. 2118.

15-yth Field Company R.E. February 1917.

Place	Date	Hour	Summary of Events and Information	Remarks and references to Appendices
KEMMEL	28/2/17		Work as usual. 3 reinforcements (Sappers) arrived. Weather - same as yesterday.	

P.A. Whitall
MAJOR, R.E.
O.C. 157th (FIELD) COMPANY R.E.

157th (FIELD) COMPANY
ROYAL ENGINEERS
1 MAR 1917

WAR DIARY
FOR MONTH OF MARCH, 1917.

VOLUME 16

UNIT:- 157th Field Company R.E.

Army Form C. 2118.

WAR DIARY
or
INTELLIGENCE SUMMARY.
(Erase heading not required.)

Instructions regarding War Diaries and Intelligence Summaries are contained in F. S. Regs., Part II. and the Staff Manual respectively. Title pages will be prepared in manuscript.

Place	Date	Hour	Summary of Events and Information	Remarks and references to Appendices
KEMMEL	1/3/17		Distribution of Work No. 1 Section - Pall Mall & Back Area.	
			" 2 " - Right Sub-sector.	
			" 3 " - Hutting.	
			" 4 " - Left Sub-sector.	
			Weather clear and fine. Wind "dangerous" - 10 a.m.	
	2/3/17		Brigade Relief. Usual inspections and lecture and demonstration by 16th Divisional Gas Officer to all ranks in camp. Weather same as yesterday.	
	3/3/17		Work as usual. Weather - slight frost in morning but thawed by sun.	
	4/3/17		Work as usual. 16th Divisional Artillery carried out operation (3.10 to 5 p.m.) advised by telephone (9.30 a.m.) that enemy seen travelling N to S over VIERSTRAAT RIDGE. Weather - same as yesterday.	

Army Form C. 2118.

WAR DIARY
or
INTELLIGENCE SUMMARY.
(Erase heading not required.)

Instructions regarding War Diaries and Intelligence Summaries are contained in F. S. Regs., Part II. and the Staff Manual respectively. Title pages will be prepared in manuscript.

Place	Date	Hour	Summary of Events and Information	Remarks and references to Appendices
KEMMEL	5/3/17		Commencement of work in line delayed till 10 am on account of operation. Weather - slight fall of snow and dull.	
	6/3/17		Work as usual. Weather - slight frost.	
	7/3/17		" " " Weather - frosty & strong easterly wind.	
	8/3/17		" " " Weather - slight frost and dull.	
	9/3/17		" " " Weather - frost broken, clear & fine	
	10/3/17		Battalion Relief. Usual inspection and practice in mess tins drill. Weather - dull and dry. C.S.M. transferred to Base. 1 Sergeant left to take up commission.	
	11/3/17		Work as usual. Weather - very mild, dull.	

Army Form C. 2118.

WAR DIARY
or
INTELLIGENCE SUMMARY.

(Erase heading not required.)

Instructions regarding War Diaries and Intelligence Summaries are contained in F. S. Regs., Part II. and the Staff Manual respectively. Title pages will be prepared in manuscript.

Place	Date	Hour	Summary of Events and Information	Remarks and references to Appendices
KEMMEL	12/3/17		No. 3 Section returned from hutting work, taking up work in Back Area.	
			Weather – dull, occasional showers of rain.	
	13/3/17		Work as usual. Weather – same as yesterday.	
	14/3/17			
	15/3/17		HQ. S.B. handed over area. Company detailed to work on Left Battalion area of 4th S.B. Work detailed as follows :-	
			No. 1 Section – O.P. at Goethals' Farm, A.D.S. Parrain Farm; providing additional billeting accommodation for sections returned from hutting.	
			No. 2 Section – Working directly under C.R.E. on wiring G.H.Q. line and Machine Gun Dugouts.	
			No. 3 Section – Front Area work.	
			No. 4 Section – Back area work; Viercourt Switch, etc. Weather – clear & fine.	

T2134. Wt. W708—776. 50000. 4/15. Sir J. C. & S.

WAR DIARY
or
INTELLIGENCE SUMMARY.
(Erase heading not required.)

Army Form C. 2118.

Place	Date	Hour	Summary of Events and Information	Remarks and references to Appendices
KEMMEL	16/3/17		Work as usual. Weather same as yesterday.	
	17/3/17		—	
	18/3/17		Usual inspections and Church Parade. Weather - same as yesterday.	
	19/3/17		Work as usual. N.C.O. left Unit for training for Commission in R.A. 2 S.M. Green joined Unit from 136th Field Co. R.E. Weather same as yesterday.	
	20/3/17		Work as usual. 2 reinforcements (Sappers) arrived. Weather - strong wind with heavy rain during night.	
	21/3/17		Work as usual. Weather - clear & fine during day; strong wind with fall of snow during night.	
	22/3/17		Work as usual. Weather - occasional heavy falls of snow. Wind "dangerous" 11.30 a.m.	

Army Form C. 2118.

WAR DIARY
or
INTELLIGENCE SUMMARY.
(Erase heading not required.)

Instructions regarding War Diaries and Intelligence Summaries are contained in F. S. Regs., Part II. and the Staff Manual respectively. Title pages will be prepared in manuscript.

Place	Date	Hour	Summary of Events and Information	Remarks and references to Appendices
KEMMEL	23/3/17		Work as usual. Weather slight frost, clear & fine	
	24/3/17		Weather same as yesterday	
	25/3/17		Rest day. Usual inspection & Church Parade. Weather same as yesterday.	
	26/3/17		Work as usual. Weather – wet & stormy. Conference reference work at L.R.E.O Office	
	27/3/17		Work as usual. Weather – wet & stormy.	
	28/3/17		Detail of Work. No. 1 Section Back Area work	
			" 2 " Front "	
			" 3 " Timber Line	
			" 4 " G.H.Q Line under L.R.E.	
			L.O.M.L.E Loteyenen Unit from 512th (London) Field Co. R.E.	
		11.30 p.m.	Message received "Test attack trench N.24.7 from FA 21A 11.17 p.m. Weather Wet.	

Army Form C. 2118.

WAR DIARY
or
INTELLIGENCE SUMMARY.
(Erase heading not required.)

Instructions regarding War Diaries and Intelligence Summaries are contained in F. S. Regs., Part II. and the Staff Manual respectively. Title pages will be prepared in manuscript.

Place	Date	Hour	Summary of Events and Information	Remarks and references to Appendices
KEMMEL	29/3/17		Work as usual. Weather - Showery. 1 Reinforcement (Driver) arrived	
	30/3/17		" " "	
	31/3/17		" " " — Casualty 1 O.R. wounded	

P. H. Hall
MAJOR, R.E.
O.C. 157th (FIELD) COMPANY R.E.

WAR DIARY FOR MONTH OF APRIL, 1917.

VOLUME:- 17

UNIT:- 137th Field Coy R.E.

WAR DIARY 15th (Field) Company, R.E.

INTELLIGENCE SUMMARY.

Army Form C. 2118.

April 1917.

(Erase heading not required.)

Instructions regarding War Diaries and Intelligence Summaries are contained in F. S. Regs., Part II. and the Staff Manual respectively. Title pages will be prepared in manuscript.

Place	Date	Hour	Summary of Events and Information	Remarks and references to Appendices
KEMMEL	1/4/17		Usual inspections and Church parade. 49th Inf. Bde. relieved 49th Inf. Bde. in line, taking over all working parties &c. Weather - fine.	
	2/4/17		O/C. R.E. (Major Marsden) visited all work of Company. Heavy fall of snow during late afternoon greatly impeding the work. Wind "dangerous" (3.20 p.m.) Organisation of work: No. 1 Section - Special work in back area. " 2 " - Front area work. " 3 " - Divisional Line. " 4 " - G.H.Q. Line under C.R.E. No. 3 Section specially strengthened and given parties of Infantry in it reliefs, each 60 strong, to push through with Divisional Line and Strong Point 14.	
	3/4/17		A blizzard stopped all work from early morning until about 3 p.m. Evening fine and full work resumed.	

WAR DIARY of 159th (Field) Company, R.E.

INTELLIGENCE SUMMARY

April 1917

Army Form C. 2118.

Place	Date	Hour	Summary of Events and Information	Remarks and references to Appendices
KEMMEL	4/4/17		Site chosen for heavy T.M. emplacement in conjunction with Divisional Trench Mortar Officer. Work interrupted on Chinese line by shelling for about 4 hours in afternoon.	
	5/4/17		Work as usual. O.C. signals showed 2nd Lieut. Leahy details of certain stations to be erected. Fine weather with showers.	
	6/4/17		Work as usual. Fine morning; wet afternoon.	
	7/4/17		Work as usual. "Gothals Horn" O.P. finished and handed over to A/177, R.F.A. 2nd Lieut. Black admitted to hospital (sick), 2nd Lieut Burke-Gaffney taking over No. 4 Section. Weather - clear & fine.	
	8/4/17		Naval inspection and Church parade.	
	9/4/17		Work as usual. Showery weather.	

WAR DIARY
or
INTELLIGENCE SUMMARY.

Army Form C. 2118.

157th (Field) Company, R.E.

April 1917.

(Erase heading not required.)

Place	Date	Hour	Summary of Events and Information	Remarks and references to Appendices
KEMMEL	10/4/17		No 1 Section transferred from work on G.H.Q. line to work on R.A. Signal dugouts and "test stations". Showery weather.	
	11/4/17		Work as usual. Showery weather.	
	12/4/17		" " " " " "	
	13/4/17		" " " " . Wind "safe" 8.25 p.m. Bright and clear day.	
	14/4/17		" " " " . Showery weather.	
	15/4/17		Usual inspections and Church parade. Wind "dangerous" 10.8 p.m. Showery weather.	
	16/4/17		Work as usual. Wind "safe" 6.45 a.m. Weather – fine in morning; wet in afternoon.	

Army Form C. 2118.

WAR DIARY
INTELLIGENCE SUMMARY

157th (Field) Company, R.E.
April 1917.

(Erase heading not required.)

Instructions regarding War Diaries and Intelligence Summaries are contained in F. S. Regs., Part II. and the Staff Manual respectively. Title pages will be prepared in manuscript.

Place	Date	Hour	Summary of Events and Information	Remarks and references to Appendices
KEMMEL	17/4/17		During last night and today work much interfered with by wet and stormy weather.	
	18/4/17		Work as usual. Advanced Dressing Station PARRAIN FARM, completed and handed over to A.D.M.S. Wind "dangerous", 8.10 pm. Showery weather.	
	19/4/17		Work as usual. Major Whittall accompanied O.C. 155th (Field) Co. R.E. round line showing him work to be taken over by his Company tomorrow. Wind "safe", 11 am. Showery weather.	
	20/4/17		Company relieved by 155th (Field) Co. R.E., No 2 Section proceeding to CLARE CAMP and remainder of Company to MONT ROUGE (Sheet 28 S.W. - M. 21. b. 7.1).	
MONT ROUGE	21/4/17 to 30/4/17		For this period two Sections were employed on hutting work and the other two on training for open warfare. 2nd Lieut. J.R. OSMOND, R.E. joined Company on 25th inst. Special attention paid to laying-out, marking & wiring strongpoints by night.	

P. Whittall
MAJOR, R.E.
O.C. 157th (FIELD) COMPANY R.E.

WAR DIARY:

VOLUME:- 18

FOR MONTH OF MAY, 1917.

UNIT:- 154th Fd. Coy. Royal Engineers

WAR DIARY 157th (Field) Company, R.E.

~~INTELLIGENCE~~ SUMMARY. May 1917

(Erase heading not required.)

Army Form C. 2118.

Place	Date	Hour	Summary of Events and Information	Remarks and references to Appendices
MONT ROUGE	1/5/17		Strength of Company: 8 Officers (1 in hospital); 213 other ranks. 2 Sections training for offensive operations, special attention being paid to laying out Strong Points by night, rapid wiring, demolition scheme, semaphore signalling, &c. 1 Section working under C.R.E. 16th Division on hutting. 1 Section working on VIERSTRAAT SWITCH and overland routes of 16th Divisional area.	
	2/5/17		Work and training same as yesterday.	
	3/5/17		" " " " " "	
	4/5/17		(5 c 1.6). Fire breaking out about 9 p.m. Enemy shelled R.E. Farm (Sh. 28 S.W.N. 15 c 1.6). Casualties: 1 Sapper killed; 1 Sapper wounded; and 1 Sapper wounded but remaining at duty.	
	5/5/17		Work and training same as yesterday.	

WAR DIARY
~~INTELLIGENCE SUMMARY~~

157th (Field) Company R.E.

May 1919.

Army Form C. 2118.

Place	Date	Hour	Summary of Events and Information	Remarks and references to Appendices
MONT ROUGE	6/5/19		Church parade and usual periodical inspections	
	7/5/19		Work and training same as yesterday. 5 reinforcements (sappers) received.	
	8/5/19		" " " " " " Major Whitehall went on leave (10th – 23rd)	
	9/5/19		" " " " " " Capt. Greenhow taking temporary command.	
	10/5/19		Work and training same as yesterday.	
	11/5/19		" " " " " " 3 Officers and 100 other ranks joined Unit for attachment for work and training	

Army Form C. 2118.

WAR DIARY
INTELLIGENCE SUMMARY.
(Erase heading not required.)

157th (Field) Company, R.E.

May 1919.

Place	Date	Hour	Summary of Events and Information	Remarks and references to Appendices
CHATHAM CAMP (LOCRE)	12/5/19		Company relieved 156th (Field) Company, R.E. in Left Sub-sector of 16th Divisional area.	
			Distribution of Company:- Headquarters, Nos. 3 and 4 Sections, and Infantry attached — CHATHAM CAMP (Sh. 28 S.W. N.23.a.8.8)	
			Nos. 1 and 2 Sections — R.E. Farm — Front line work.	
			Work in back area.	
	13/5/19		Work as yesterday.	
	14/5/19		" " "	
	15/5/19		1 W.O. joined Company on transfer from 156th (Field) Co. R.E.	
	16/5/19		1 reinforcement (Sapper) arrived.	

WAR DIARY 157th (Field) Company, R.E. Army Form C. 2118.

INTELLIGENCE SUMMARY. May 1917.

(Erase heading not required.)

Place	Date	Hour	Summary of Events and Information	Remarks and references to Appendices
HATHAM CAMP	17/5/17.		Work as usual.	
	18/5/17.		" " "	
	19/5/17.		" " "	
	20/5/17.		" " "	
	21/5/17.		" " " . 1 W.S.O. and 1 Sapper awarded Military medal for work in connection with fire at Pte. Noeux (referred to above).	
	22/5/17.		Work as usual. 1 reinforcement (W.S.O.) received.	
	23/5/17.		" " "	

T2134. Wt. W708-776. 500000. 4/15. Sir J. C. & S.

Army Form C. 2118.

WAR DIARY

INTELLIGENCE SUMMARY.

157th (Field) Company R.E.

May 1917.

(Erase heading not required.)

Place	Date	Hour	Summary of Events and Information	Remarks and references to Appendices
CHATHAM CAMP.	24/5/17		Work as usual. Wind "safe". 9.5 a.m. Major Whithall returned from leave. Transport moved from LOCRE to MONT ROUGE.	
	25/5/17		Work as usual. Wind "dangerous". 4.45 p.m. Beauvallio onward attacked: 1 killed, 1 wounded; 1 wounded – at duty; 1 shell shock.	
	26/5/17		Work as usual.	
	27/5/17		" " " Beauvallio: 1 Driver killed; 2 horses and 1 mule killed; 2 mules wounded.	
	28/5/17		Work as usual.	
	29/5/17		" " " 9.35 a.m. Beauvallio; 1 attached man wounded. Wind "safe".	

Army Form C. 2118.

WAR DIARY

INTELLIGENCE SUMMARY

157th (Field) Company R.E.

May 1917.

(Erase heading not required.)

Place	Date	Hour	Summary of Events and Information	Remarks and references to Appendices
CHATHAM CAMP.	30/5/17		Work as usual.	
	31/5/17		— " — " — " — " — " —	
			Strength of Company: 8 Officers (1 in hospital); 211 other ranks.	

P. Whittall
MAJOR, R.E.
O.C. 157th (FIELD) COMPANY R.E.

WAR DIARY.

FOR MONTH OF JUNE, 1917.

VOLUME:- 19

UNIT:- 157th Field Company R.E.

Army Form C. 2118.

154th Field Company R.E.

WAR DIARY

~~INTELLIGENCE~~ SUMMARY.

(Erase heading not required.)

June 1917.

Instructions regarding War Diaries and Intelligence Summaries are contained in F. S. Regs., Part II. and the Staff Manual respectively. Title pages will be prepared in manuscript.

Place	Date	Hour	Summary of Events and Information	Remarks and references to Appendices
CHATHAM CAMP.	1/6/17		Strength of Company: 8 Officers (1 in hospital). 211 other ranks. Distribution of Work. No. 1 & 2 Sections - Front line work on left sub. sector of 16th Divisional area. - both sections living at R.E. FARM. No. 3 & 4 Sections. Work in back area.	
		4 p.m	No. 1 & 3 Sections, completed all work detailed by C.R.E. for completion by 1st June, & returned to Headquarters at CHATHAM CAMP. No. 3 Section moved to R.E. FARM, for work on ordinary Trench maintenance &c. 1 O.R. succumbed.	
	2/6/17		2 Sections resting. 1 Section on Trench maintenance & 1 Section on work in back area. 48th Infantry Brigade relieved by 49th and 149th Infantry Brigades, in left sub. sector.	
	3/6/17		Work as for 2nd instant 1 O.R. to hospital (sick) 3 O.R. join as reinforcements.	

Army Form C. 2118.

WAR DIARY
INTELLIGENCE SUMMARY.
(Erase heading not required.)

157th Field Company R.E.
June 1917.

Place	Date	Hour	Summary of Events and Information	Remarks and references to Appendices
CHATHAM CAMP.	4/6/17		3. Sections training in Camp. 1. Section still on Trench maintenance. 1. O.R. granted leave to U.K. Strength of Company 8 Officers (1 in hospital) 213 O.R.	
	5/6/17		3. Sections short route march, games etc. regarding each Sections duties in offensive operations. 2. O.R. take part in raid by 49th Infantry Brigade for demolitions.	
		5pm	Company Commanders conference with 6 R.E. (notification of award of D.S.O. to Major R.J. WHITTALL RE (O.C. Coy)	
	6/6/17		All parades cancelled. Company ordered to stand by. 1. O.R. to hospital (sick)	
		6.40pm	Company Operation Order issued (copy attached)	

Army Form C. 2118.

WAR DIARY
or
INTELLIGENCE SUMMARY.
(Erase heading not required.)

Place	Date	Hour	Summary of Events and Information	Remarks and references to Appendices
CHATHAM CAMP.	6/7	MID-NIGHT 12	The Company (less 1 Section) tolerks lumbers, a party of 65 attached Infantry and a specially formed Pack Train of 20 mules, left CHATHAM CAMP at midnight 6th/7th June & proceeded to R.E. FARM, in the neighbourhood of which, they took up assembly positions. They were in position by 1.50 a.m. 7th June. No 1 Section had proceeded to SHANTUNG with 3S attached Infantry under orders of G.O.C. 49th Infantry Brigade. ORDER OF BATTLE & POSITIONS. O.C. MAJOR P.F. WHITTALL R.E. with 49th Infy. Bde. Hd. Qrs. 2nd in C. CAPT E.K. GREENHOW R.E. i/c Brigade Transport & Divisional R.E. at CANADA CORNER. No 1 SECTION 2ND LT G.H. BAXTER R.E. " 2 " 2ND LT W.J. LEAHY R.E. " 3 " LIEUT C.N.B. BOLTON R.E. " 4 " 2ND LT E. O'D BURKE-GAFFNEY R.E. Spare Officer :- 2ND LT J.R. OSMOND R.E. i/c Mule Pack Train	

WAR DIARY or INTELLIGENCE SUMMARY

154th Field Company R.E.

June 1917.

Place	Date	Hour	Summary of Events and Information	Remarks and references to Appendices
	1/6/17		ATTACHED INFANTRY.	

"RED" PARTY.   2ND LT. P.H. FIGGIS. 7/8TH ROYAL IRISH FUSILIERS
"BLACK" PARTY.   2ND LT. F.M. EAGER. — DO —
"ODD" PARTY.   2ND LT. ROCHE. 2ND ROYAL IRISH REGIMENT.

ORGANISATION

The Company was arranged to work in Sections except 1 N.C.O and 8 men, withdrawn from No 4 Section, to pack and unload the Pack Mule train for R.E. stores.

The pack mule train was improvised out of the Company Transport with 16 additional pack saddles specially issued.

The attached Infantry were told off into three parties:-
"RED" PARTY under   2ND LT. P.H. FIGGIS. 7/8TH ROYAL IRISH FUSILIERS
"BLACK"   "   2ND LT. F.M. EAGER.   ",,   ",,
"ODD"   "   2ND LT. ROCHE. 2ND ROYAL IRISH REGT.

These were attached respectively to No 1, 2 & 3 Sections, with

Army Form C. 2118.

15th Field Co. R.E.

June 1917

WAR DIARY
INTELLIGENCE SUMMARY.
(Erase heading not required.)

Place	Date	Hour	Summary of Events and Information	Remarks and references to Appendices
	1/6/17		In area Kati.	
			No. 1 Section could dig and wire "RED" POST.	
			" 2 " " " " " "BLACK"	
			" 3 " - arrange the filling of forward dumps for R.E. material.	
		4.00am	OPERATIONS. Under instructions from G.O.C. 49th Infantry Brigade, O.C. ordered No. 2 Section & "BLACK" party to move up from R.E. FARM to proposed site for "BLACK" post. O.C. then proceeded to SHANTUNG & took No. 1 Section & "RED" party up with	
		8.15am	him, sited "RED" POST and left them at work.	
		8.30am	O.C. sited "BLACK" POST, marked it, and returned with a guide, and meeting No. 2 Section in our own advanced trenches in his return, handed over the guide. "BLACK" party was reported as following, but was afterwards discovered, to have been scattered by shell fire, the men returning to R.E. FARM, whence they were meanwhile ordered forward.	

Army Form C. 2118.

WAR DIARY
of
INTELLIGENCE SUMMARY.
(Erase heading not required.)

157th Field Company R.E.

June 1917.

Place	Date	Hour	Summary of Events and Information	Remarks and references to Appendices
	1/6/17	9.30am	Mule teams moved forward & began work of forming dump as near to "BLACK" Post as possible.	
		10.10am	O.C. returned to Brigade H.Q. and arrived remainder of Company & Infantry up to R.I.B. (Brigade Hd. Qrs.) from R.E. FARM	
		10.55am	Three parties arrived and began moving stores from Intermediate dump to WATSONVILLE DUMP, and strengthening bridge next the LAITERIE to take 6 tonners.	
		11.15am	Specially rebuilding a bridge next the LAITERIE to take 6 tonners.	
			also the VIERSTRAAT SWITCH Bridge finished.	
		1.50pm		
		4pm	No. 3 Section and remaining Infantry move forward to pick up No. 1 & 2 sections and all proceed to make OBVIOUS POST. Lieut. BOLTON detailed to search for water, and if possible install pumps and take samples for testing.	
		5pm	"RED" POST completed.	
		6pm	"BLACK" POST completed.	
		9.35pm	OBVIOUS Sir J.C. POST completed.	

Army Form C. 2118.

WAR DIARY
or
INTELLIGENCE SUMMARY.

(Erase heading not required.)

157th Field Company R.E.

June 1914

Place	Date	Hour	Summary of Events and Information	Remarks and references to Appendices
	7/6/17	11.35pm	All sections, Infantry & Pack train withdrawn to BEAVER FARM for the night.	
BEAVER FARM	8/6/17	10.00am	No. 4 Section proved to join up "RED", "BLACK" and "OBVIOUS" POSTS with a hand & wire.	
			No. 3 section with Infantry proved to continue with the Pack train to move R.E. stores forward on foot as possible, and continue search for water.	
		5.0pm	Wire laid, above referred to, completed.	
		5.30pm	WYTSCHAETE Village Well fitted with a pump, and one other well discovered.	
			On completion of above tasks, the Company reformed at BEAVER FARM, by about 9.30 p.m.	
	9/6/17		Company returns to CHATHAM CAMP	

Army Form C. 2118.

WAR DIARY
or
INTELLIGENCE SUMMARY.
(Erase heading not required.)

Instructions regarding War Diaries and Intelligence Summaries are contained in F. S. Regs., Part II. and the Staff Manual respectively. Title pages will be prepared in manuscript.

Place	Date	Hour	Summary of Events and Information	Remarks and references to Appendices
CHATHAM CAMP	10/6/17		Usual inspections & Church Parades 2/Lieut BAXTER granted leave.	
	11/6/17		Company rest	
	12/6/17		"	
	13/6/17		Company & attached Infantry leave CHATHAM CAMP & make camp on YORK ROAD.	
YORK RD.	14/6/17		Work on WYTSCHAETE RIDGE defences.	
	15/6/17			
	16/6/17		Lieut BOLTON granted leave.	
	17/6/17		Usual inspections & Church Parade.	
	18/6/17		Company leaves YORK RD. at 9.0 am & proceeds via Route "A" and	

WAR DIARY
INTELLIGENCE SUMMARY.
(Erase heading not required.)

Army Form C. 2118.

157th Field Company R.E.

June 1917

Place	Date	Hour	Summary of Events and Information	Remarks and references to Appendices
METEREN to MERRIS				
MERRIS	19/6/17		First day for Company. Attached Infantry rejoin their own units. 2/Lieut. J.C. BLACK rejoins Unit from hospital.	
	20/6/17		Company leave MERRIS at 8.0 a.m. & proceed to EECKE.	
EECKE	21/6/17		Journey continued from EECKE at 5.30 a.m. to POPERINGHE via STEENVOORDE & ABEELE.	
POPERINGHE	22/6/17 23/6/17		Making camp and training	
	24/6/17 to 30/6/17		2/Lieut. STEVENSON, R.J. proceeds to England 24.6.17 for advice up to Officer Cadet Unit. Company employed in sorting Ammunition Dumps augg. eng. 2/Lieut. G.L. GREENHOW R.E. granted leave 27.6.17. Strength of Company 8 Officers; 204 other ranks.	

P.H. Heath
MAJOR, R.E.
O.C. 157th (FIELD) COMPANY R.E.

SECRET.

157th. FIELD COMPANY R.E. OPERATION ORDER No. 1.

6th. June 1917.

1. The dismounted portion of the Company (less H1. Qrs) with Attached Infantry and 20 pack mules will move into assembly positions to-night.

2. No. 1 Section and "Red" Party of Attached Infantry (35 strong) will be on YORK ROAD ready to enter "FOSSE" C.T. at 11.10 p.m. and proceed via FOSSE C.T. and R.P. 13 to SHANTUNG where they will await orders to move, which will come from O.C. Coy.

3. 3 Tool Cart Teams and 3 Limbers will be at Camp by 11.45 p.m. for hooking in and loading, also 1 Limber loaded with 1 day's forage for 20 mules. They will return to-night on completion of move.

4. Nos. 2, 3 and 4 Sections, with balance of Attached Infantry will parade at 11.55 p.m. and proceed by Sections (complete with Tool Cart and Limber) at intervals of 100 yards via Route "A", HUT ROAD, BUFFER CROSSING, Route "F" and MILKY WAY to the Assembly Positions appointed in O.R.Q.11, E. of R.E. FARM.

5. The 20 pack mules will be under 2/Lt OSMOND who will be shown where to picket them. If possible they should be picketted in groups of not more than 4 in any one place.

6. Completion of move to be reported by code word PIXY to C. R. E.

7. Company H.Q. will move forward consequent on advance of working parties to PARROT TRENCH. Such move will be ordered by O.C. and will be reported to C. R. E.
Sections returning from work in first place will halt in CHINESE LINE between WATLING and SNOW SCRAPES to await further orders.

8. O.C., Coy. will be with 49th. I.B., H.Q.

9. Rations for to-morrow and complete Iron Rations are to be carried by every man.

10. East of YORK ROAD all Box Respirators are to be worn in alert position.

11. Subsequent orders as to moves have been forecasted and will be issued by O.C.

Issued at 6.40 p.m.

R. F. Whittall
Major R.E.
O.C. 157th. (Field) Coy. R.E.

Copies to all
    Officers.

WAR DIARY.

FOR MONTH OF JULY, 1917.

VOLUME :- 20

UNIT :- 154th Field Coy RE

Army Form C. 2118.

WAR DIARY
INTELLIGENCE SUMMARY.

of 154th Field Company R.E.
July 1917.

(Erase heading not required.)

Instructions regarding War Diaries and Intelligence Summaries are contained in F. S. Regs., Part II. and the Staff Manual respectively. Title pages will be prepared in manuscript.

Place	Date	Hour	Summary of Events and Information	Remarks and references to Appendices
POPERINGHE.	11th to 12th		Company employed on sinking wells in administrative area.	
	13th		Drill in morning. Baths in afternoon.	
	14th		Men's inspections.	
	15th		Company leaves POPERINGHE and joins 49th Infantry Brigade Group at WINNIZEELE. 2nd Lieut BURKE-GAFFNEY granted leave to U.K.	
WINNIZEELE	16th		Company training. 2nd Lieut BAXTER admitted to hospital (sick) L.R.E.'s Order announces award of Military Medals to Lance-Corporals BOOTHROYD and JERRAM, and Military Cross to 2nd Lieut. LEAHY.	

Army Form C. 2118.

WAR DIARY
of 157th Field Company R.E.
~~INTELLIGENCE SUMMARY.~~
(Erase heading not required.)

July 1917

Instructions regarding War Diaries and Intelligence Summaries are contained in F. S. Regs., Part II. and the Staff Manual respectively. Title pages will be prepared in manuscript.

Place	Date	Hour	Summary of Events and Information	Remarks and references to Appendices
WINNIZEELE.	17th		Company Training. 1. O.R. joins as reinforcement.	
	18th		Company Training	
	19th		Company Training. 2nd Lieut OSMOND and 10 O.R. to Fifth Army Rest Camp.	
	20th 23rd		Company Training	
	24th		Company Training. 1. Officer & 51 O.R. 1/8th Royal Irish Fusiliers attached.	
	25th		Company Training	
	26th		Leave WINNIZEELE and proceed to WATOU area.	

Army Form C. 2118.

WAR DIARY
or
INTELLIGENCE SUMMARY.
(Erase heading not required.)

157th Field Company R.E.
July 1917.

Instructions regarding War Diaries and Intelligence Summaries are contained in F. S. Regs., Part II. and the Staff Manual respectively. Title pages will be prepared in manuscript.

Place	Date	Hour	Summary of Events and Information	Remarks and references to Appendices
WATOU	27th 28th		Company training.	
	29th		Company training. 3.O.R. join as reinforcements.	
	30th		Company training.	
	31st	12.15am	Leave WATOU area for assembly position at SHEET 28 N.W. G.11.d.1.5 (on POPERINGHE - YPRES ROAD) Company standing to, awaiting orders. 2nd Lieut OSMOND rejoins from Fifth Army Rest Camp.	

C. H. Nuttall
MAJOR, R.E.
O.C. 157th (FIELD) COMPANY R.E.

WAR DIARY.

FOR MONTH OF AUGUST, 1917.

VOLUME 21

UNIT 157th Field Company R.E.

Vol 21

Army Form C. 2118.

WAR DIARY 154th Field Company R.E.
or
INTELLIGENCE SUMMARY. August 1917.
(Erase heading not required.)

Place	Date	Hour	Summary of Events and Information	Remarks and references to Appendices
	1st to 3rd		Company at G.11.d.1.5 (Ref 28) awaiting orders. Very bad weather.	
	4th	10 PM	Lewis above position & proceed to BRANDHOEK N° 1 & 2 Dugouts & Stables Infantry continue journey to YPRES & billet in the Ramparts. Employed on general preparation for the Offensive, move & work forming advanced dump of R.E. Stores & preparing new cross country tracks to replace those ruined by bad weather.	
	5th		As above. 1-O.R. wounded in action	
	6th		As above. 1-O.R. wounded in action & 6 O.R. evacuated.	
	7th & 8th		As above	
	9th		As above. 1-O.R. joined as reinforcement.	

WAR DIARY
or
INTELLIGENCE SUMMARY

157th Field Company R.E.
August 1917

Place	Date	Hour	Summary of Events and Information	Remarks and references to Appendices
	10th		As above. 2nd Lt. W J LEAHY RE wounded in action. 2nd Lt. P H FIGGIS (Royal Irish Fusiliers attached) wounded in action. 1 Officer and 50 O.R. Connaught Rangers join in attachment.	
	11th		Work as above.	
	12th		No 3 & 4 Sections attached Infantry Connaught Rangers. Relieve No 1 & 2 Sections and attached Royal Irish Fusiliers in YPRES. 19 O.R. join as reinforcements. 1 O.R. wounded (at duty). 2 O.R. wounded in action.	
	13th		2nd Lieut. G. A. BAXTER returns from hospital. 1 O.R. wounded in action.	
	14th		1 O.R. wounded in action.	

WAR DIARY / INTELLIGENCE SUMMARY

15th Field Company R.E.

August 1917

Date	Hour	Summary of Events and Information	Remarks
15th	6.15pm	Remainder of the dismounted portion of the Company including an improvised section of 30 numbers (less details) moved to advanced C of R in H.18.A as per Operation Order attached.	
	11.0pm	Left H.6.A for assembly position allotted in old GERMAN front line. 1 O.R. wounded.	
16th	2.15am	Assembly completed.	
	11.0pm	Nos. 3 & 4 Sections proceeded to try and strengthen SQUARE FARM but were unable to do so owing to extremely heavy enemy shelling. No.1 Section stayed in GERMAN front line in support to the other two Sections, but had to move back to old BRITISH front line, to make room for a Support Battalion.	
17th	4.0am	Nos. 3 & 4 Sections returned and joined other Sections	

WAR DIARY or INTELLIGENCE SUMMARY.

Army Form C. 2118.

154th Field Company R.E.

August 1917.

Place	Date	Hour	Summary of Events and Information	Remarks and references to Appendices
			at Coventry Rations	
		1.30pm	Sections left Coventry Rations and returned to H.18.A.	
		6.30pm	Company, less No. 2 Section and attached Infantry returned to BRANDHOEK. 2 O.R. Killed and 3 O.R. wounded. Lieut. J. M. J. HAUGHTON join Company for duty.	
	18	3 P.M.	No. 2 Section relieved in YPRES and rejoin remainder of Company at BRANDHOEK	
	19	6.am	Company left BRANDHOEK and march to W7OU "C" area. attached Infantry rejoined their own Battalions	
	20		Company marched to GODWAERSVELDE.	

Army Form C. 2118.

Instructions regarding War Diaries and Intelligence Summaries are contained in F. S. Regs., Part II. and the Staff Manual respectively. Title pages will be prepared in manuscript.

WAR DIARY
OF 157th Field Company R.E.
INTELLIGENCE SUMMARY.
(Erase heading not required.)

August 1917.

Place	Date	Hour	Summary of Events and Information	Remarks and references to Appendices
	21st	9.30am	Company marched to CASSELL (BAVINCHOVE STATION)	
		4.20pm	Entrainment completed and train started	
	22nd	2.0am	Detrained at MIRAUMONT and marched to ACHIET-LE-PETIT	
ACHIET-LE-PETIT	23rd 24th 25th		Company training	
	26th		Inspection of Divisional R.E. by G.O.C. Division. 1 O.R. joins as reinforcements	
	27th	9.30am	Company marched from ACHIET-LE-PETIT to HAMELINCOURT	
HAMELINCOURT	28th 29th 30th 31st		No. 1, 3 & 4 Sections employed on hutting and No. 2 Section at Divisional Dump	

P. H. Kittall
MAJOR, R.E.
O.C. 157th (FIELD) COMPANY R.E.

SECRET

Copy No. 8

OPERATION ORDERS BY O.C. 157th. (FIELD) COY. R.E.

15th. August 1917.

1. At 6.0 p.m. to-day, Nos. 1 and 2 Sections with attached Infantry of 49th. Inf. Bde. will march to H.18.a. and bivouac, taking tool carts, limbers, watercart and G.S. Wagon with Pack Saddles and boxes. The G.S. Wagon will return to Camp when unloaded. Dress - Marching Order with one extra water bottle.

2. At 11.0 p.m. the above party less transport will parade to march to Assembly Position. Dress - Marching Order less Packs. Haversacks to be carried as packs and two water bottles to be carried filled.
Nos. 3 and 4 Sections with attached Infantry of 47th. Inf. Bde. will be ready to join the Company at MENIN GATE at 11.30 p.m. Cooks to be left behind at this move.

3. MEALS. Tea in Camp at 4.30 p.m. Supper in bivouac at 8.30 p.m. with a Rum issue.
Each man on move detailed in 2, is to carry rations for 16th. and Iron Rations.
After the Company has moved off at 11.0 p.m., cooks will be responsible for keeping hot water always ready so that any party can be sent back for hot tea either to the RAMPARTS or bivouac.

4. ASSEMBLY POSITIONS AND ORGANISATION FOR WORK.

At I.5.b.
(a) No. 1 Section with 30 attached Infantry from 49th. Inf. Bde.
(b) No. 3 Section with 30 attached Infantry from 47th. Inf. Bde.
(c) No. 4 Section with 5 attached Infantry from each 47th. and 49th. Inf. Bdes.

In RAMPARTS. in Reserve. No. 2 Section with balance of attached Infantry in reserve. Section Officer to keep in touch with Lt JENNINGS. R.E. at Advanced D.H.Q.

Sergt. LOW J.P. with a Guard of 3 men from No. 2 Section will remain at H.18.a.

O.C., with orderlies will be at Bde. H.Q., MILL COT.

On the order being given to proceed to work :-

(a) Will proceed to work detailed on attached Table at IBERIAN FARM.

(b) Will proceed to work detailed on attached Table at DELVA FARM.

(c) Will proceed to work detailed on attached Table on bridges and approaches.

In the event of any occurrence preventing any of the above parties from commencing or carrying on work, a message is at once to be sent to O.C., at MILL COT.
A report should also be sent in when it is estimated that one more hour's work will finish the work, so that fresh instructions can be issued if necessary, but in the event of no other orders being received when work is done, the party will return to assembly position in I.5.b., reporting arrival.

5. STORES.   All stores required are to be drawn from SIX TREES Dump on way up to work, and if necessary, carrying parties from attached Infantry organised and sent back for more.

6. REPORT CENTRES. O.C. 157th. (Field) Coy. R.E.   MILL COT.
                    Advanced H.Q., R.E.   RAMPARTS.I.8.d.1.8
                    H.Q., R.E.   H.7.d.0.4.

Issued at 2.30pm

P. F. Whittall
Major R.E.
O.C. 157th. (Field) Coy. R.E.

Copy No. 1 O.C. No. 1 Section.   Copy No. 5 Second-in-Command.
         2 O.C. No. 2 Section.   6 O.C. Company.
         3 O.C. No. 3 Section.   7 & 8. War Diary.
         4 O.C. No. 4 Section.

TABLE OF WORK.

No. 1 Section with 30 Infantry :-

      IBERIAN FARM, D.19.b.2.2.

No. 3 Section with 30 Infantry :-

      DELVA FARM, D.20.a.05.30.

To be made into supporting points.
    A wire fence to be put up in front first and on flanks afterwards if possible.
    Where there are concrete dug-outs the exposed extrances will be traversed with sandbag wall and bursters.
    Where no dugouts exist the main building will be wired in and protection added to any existing cellar.
    Notches and embrasures for Lewis Guns will be made adjacent to dugouts and cellars.

No. 4 Section with 10 Infantry :-

(1) Repair existing bridges, or new bridges to take pack mules will be put in, over the STEENBECK at D.19.d.1.T., D.19.c.45.70 and D.19.c.40.80.

(2) Repair existing bridges for Infantry or put in light Infantry bridges over STEENBECK at D.19.d.75.20 (2) and D.19.d.35.45 and over ZONNEBEKE at D.20.c.10.65 (where Tramway crosses.)

    Each Section will detail a man to search for dumps of enemy R.E. Stores and report any found.

P. F. Whittall

                      Major R.E.
          O.C. 157th. (Field) Coy. R.E.

WAR DIARY.

FOR MONTH OF SEPTEMBER, 1917.

VOLUME 22

UNIT:- 15th Fd Co RE

CONFIDENTIAL.

WAR DIARY

OF

157th. (FIELD) COMPANY R.E.

from 1st. September 1917 to 30th. September 1917.

WAR DIARY or INTELLIGENCE SUMMARY

Army Form C. 2118.

134th Field Company R.E. September 1917

Place	Date	Hour	Summary of Events and Information	Remarks and references to Appendices
HAMELINCOURT	1st		Entire Company at H.Q. O.C. went on leave to U.K. Capt Greenhow took over temporary command of Company. No 3 Section proceeded to BEHAGNIES to work on new Divisional H.Q.	
	2nd		No 1 & 2 Sections proceeded to Quarry Billets for work on Eighth Subsection Shaft. Lieut Ashworth 16th Durham Light Inf. Work taken over from O.C. 155 Field Company R.E. No 4 Section started on Battalion dugouts report.	
	3rd		2nd Lt Burke Gaffney proceeded to ETAPLES to report to C.R.E. for work.	
	4th		2nd Lt J. R. Osmond rejoined from leave.	
	5th		Lieut H.N.S. Haughton wounded in action. 1 O.R. wounded in action (gas). Lt Moreton joined from Base. 1 O.R. joined from Base.	
	6th & 14th		Work as above.	
	15th		Company assembled at Company H.Q. 2nd Lt A.H. Glynn joined from 155 Field Coy R.E.	
	16th		No 3 & 4 Sections took over work on line & Advanced Billets. No 2 Section on Hutting near Adjutant R.E. but remain billeted at Company H.Q.	
	17th & 21st		Work as above.	
	22nd		2 O.R. wounded in action (gas)	
	23rd		O.C. rejoined from leave	
	24th		O.C. attached to Divisional H.Q. as acting C.R.E.	
	25th & 28th		Work as above.	

WAR DIARY
or
INTELLIGENCE SUMMARY.

Army Form C. 2118.

157th Field Company R.E.

Place	Date	Hour	Summary of Events and Information	Remarks and references to Appendices
HAMELINCOURT	29th 30th		Company assembled at Company HQ. Recent awards acting C.R.E. of Military Medal Ribbons to:- No. 46290 Sergt. C.G. BIRD. No. 3343 2/Cpl. J. REEVES. No. 134467 L/Cpl. J. ALLAN. No. 94193 Sapper J. BLACKBURN. No. 108788 Sapper J.P. COYNE. No. 32489 Dr. A.M. ERSKINE. No. 136727 Driver T. GARDNER. No. 1 + 2 Sections still over work in line + Advanced Billets and No. 4 Section tutting under Adjutant R.E.	

Signature, Capt. R.E.
for O.C. 157th Field Co. R.E.

[Stamp: 157TH FIELD COMPANY ROYAL ENGINEERS 2 OCT 1917]

Wiring Organisation.

2 Companies of Infantry. — 800 Yards.

Drill II — Double Concertina.

- 1 - R.E. Officer.
- 1 - R.E. Sergeant.

Left Company
1 - Company Commander R.I. Regt.

- 1 - Officer
  - 4 - Parties (1,2,3,4)
  - Each 1 - N.C.O.
  - 1 - Sapper.
  - 7 - Men.
- 1 - Officer
  - 4 - Parties (5,6,7,8)
  - Each 1 - N.C.O.
  - 1 - Sapper.
  - 7 - Men.

Right Company
1 - Company Commander R.I. Fus.

- 1 - Officer
  - 4 - Parties (9,10,11,12)
  - Each 1 - N.C.O.
  - 1 - Sapper.
  - 7 - Men.
- 1 - Officer
  - 4 - Parties (13,14,15,16)
  - Each 1 - N.C.O.
  - 1 - Sapper.
  - 7 - Men.

800 Yards divided into 16 Tasks of 50 Yards each.

↓ ENEMY.

2-9-17

P.K. Whittall, Major R.E.
O.C. 157th (Field) Coy. R.E.

WAR DIARY

FOR MONTH OF OCTOBER, 1917.

UNIT 157th Field Coy R.E.

VOLUME NUMBER 23

Vol 23

CONFIDENTIAL.

WAR DIARY

OF

157th. (FIELD) COMPANY R. E.

from 1st. October 1917   to   31st. October 1917.

Army Form C. 2118.

WAR DIARY
INTELLIGENCE SUMMARY.
(Erase heading not required.)

157th (Field) Company R.E.

October 1917

Place	Date	Hour	Summary of Events and Information	Remarks and references to Appendices
HAMELINCOURT	1st		Company working in Eight Sub. sections of 16th Divisional Front. Lt. L.M.A.O. GREEN Signal Engineer to H.Q. R.E. with effect from 19.8.17. 2nd Lieut E.N. BANCROFT joined for duty from C.E. XVII CORPS. Lieut F.H. MONCKTON Transferred to C.E. XVII CORPS.	
	2nd			
	3rd		Work as above.	
	4th			
	5th		3. O.R. joined as reinforcements.	
	6th		Work as above	
	8th			
	9th		1. O.R joined as reinforcement.	
	10th		O.I. Company rejoined from H.Q. R.E.	

Army Form C. 2118.

WAR DIARY
INTELLIGENCE SUMMARY

(Erase heading not required.)

154th (Field) Company R.E.
October 1917

Place	Date	Hour	Summary of Events and Information	Remarks and references to Appendices
	11th		Work as above.	
	12th			
	13th		No 1 & 2 Sections left advanced Billets and rejoined Company Headquarters.	
	14th		Rest day, with usual Personal Inspections and Church Parade. No 3 & 4 Sections moved to Advanced Billets.	
	15th		Work as above.	
	16th			
	17th		2nd Lieut G.H. BAXTER granted leave to U.K.	
	18th		Work as above.	
	19th			
	24th			
	25th		O.C. attended Field Company Commanders' con-	

Army Form C. 2118.

WAR DIARY
or
INTELLIGENCE SUMMARY.

157th (Field) Company R.E.
October 1917

(Erase heading not required.)

Instructions regarding War Diaries and Intelligence Summaries are contained in F. S. Regs., Part II. and the Staff Manual respectively. Title pages will be prepared in manuscript.

Place	Date	Hour	Summary of Events and Information	Remarks and references to Appendices
	26th		Service with C.R.E.	
	27th		Work as above.	
	28th		Captain E. R. GREENHOW granted leave to U.K. Rest day with usual Divisional Inspections and Church Parades. No 1 & 2 Sections moved to new advanced Billets in CROISILLES CAVES.	
	29th		2nd Lieut G.H. BAXTER rejoined from leave. Work as above	
	30th		2nd Lieut E O'D. BURKE-GAFFNEY struck off the strength of Company.	
	31st		C.S.M. J.O FAHY joined for duty from Base	

P. Whittall
MAJOR, R.E.
O.C. 157th (FIELD) COMPANY R.E.

WAR DIARY

FOR MONTH OF NOVEMBER, 1917.

VOLUME :- 24

UNIT :- 154th Labour Bn.

Army Form C. 2118.

WAR DIARY
or
INTELLIGENCE SUMMARY.
(Erase heading not required.)

151st (Field) Company R.E.

November 1917.

Place	Date	Hour	Summary of Events and Information	Remarks and references to Appendices
HAMELINCOURT	1st		Company working on Right Sub Section & Left Section of 16th Divisional Front. No 1 Section (less certain details) were relieved on Advanced Billets by No 4 Section	
	2nd to 8th		No 1 Section training 2 Special Mining Companies & 2nd Royal Irish Regiment and 11th Royal Irish Fusiliers, and No 3 Section training French Blocking & digging parties. Capt R.L. Greenhow rejoined from leave on 8th.	
	9th		No 1 Section proceeded to Advanced Billets and relieved No 4 Section, who returned to Company Headquarters. 1 O.R. joined Company on attachment from 151st (Field) Company R.E. with a view to transfer.	
	10th 11th 12th		No 1 Section were employed in stocking Advanced Dumps. Lt Col R.E. inspected Camp at Company Headquarters on 11th.	
	13th		No 3 Section relieved No 1 Section in Advanced Billets and carried on the work of stocking Advanced Dumps. No 1 Section returned to Headquarters – continued	

Army Form C. 2118.

WAR DIARY
or
INTELLIGENCE SUMMARY.— 151st (Field) Coy R.E.

(Erase heading not required.)

November 1917.

Instructions regarding War Diaries and Intelligence Summaries are contained in F. S. Regs., Part II. and the Staff Manual respectively. Title pages will be prepared in manuscript.

Place	Date	Hour	Summary of Events and Information	Remarks and references to Appendices
	14th to 17th		The training of Infantry Mining Companies	
	18th		Work as above	
			1 - O.R. transferred to R.E. Base Depot. No. 1 Section relieved No. 2 Section who, with all attached Infantry, returned to Company H.Q.	
	19th		Attached Tunnelling Personnel reported Company 3 - O.R. joined as reinforcements	
	20th	2.30 p.m	Advanced Company Headquarters established in CROISILLE CAVES. In accordance with attached Operation Order N° 1 & 3 Sections went in assembly positions with Mining & digging parties by 5.30 am. At 6.20 am (ZERO Hour) the attack took place, and the operations took their normal course in accordance with instructions, except on the left, where all the mine could not be completed. It was however completed	

WAR DIARY
or
INTELLIGENCE SUMMARY.

(Erase heading not required.)

151st (Field) Company Army Form C. 2118.

November 1917

Place	Date	Hour	Summary of Events and Information	Remarks and references to Appendices
			Last night. The nightly Coy Reporting Battalion of the 49th I.B. reported completion of their belt of wire at 7.8 am. Both the new Communication Trenches were in use within 3½ hours of ZERO.	
			CASUALTIES	
			2nd Lt. G.H. BAXTER Wounded (at duty)	
			1. O.R. Killed	
			2. O.R. Wounded.	
			No. 3 Section proceeded to Advanced Billets and relieved No. 1 Section.	
	22nd		No. 3 Section returned to Advanced - Billets and No. 1 Section returned to Company Headquarters leaving only a Section in Advanced Billets. Company Headquarters Advanced. 2nd Lt. E.N. BANCROFT took over command of No. 2 Section from 2nd Lt. T.C. GLYNN	
	23rd		Work as above.	

WAR DIARY or INTELLIGENCE SUMMARY

Army Form C. 2118.

157th (Field) Company R.E.

November 1917.

Place	Date	Hour	Summary of Events and Information	Remarks and references to Appendices
	24th		No 4 Section proceeded to unnamed Billets. No 1 Section with wiring Companies as in previous Operation. Put out additional Belt of Wire at night. I.O.R joined as reinforcement.	
	25th 26th		Work as above.	
	27th		1.O.R. Killed in action. 1.O.R. wounded in action. 2ND LT E N BANCROFT granted leave to U.K. 2ND LT. T. C. GLYNN assumed command of No 2 Section.	
	28th 29th		Work as above.	
	30		No. 1 & 3 Sections to advanced Billets & No. 2 Section returned to Company Headquarters.	

P A Whittall
MAJOR, R.E.
O.C. 157th (FIELD) COMPANY, R.E.

SECRET.

No 9

157th. (FIELD) COMPANY R.E.

OPERATION ORDER No. 1 of 19th. November 1917.

1.   Certain Operations are being carried out by VI Corps on a day which will be known as "Z" Day.   "Z" day and Zero hour will be notified to all concerned later.

        The Company will work with 49th. I.B.

2.   On Y/Z night the Company will be disposed as follows :-

Company Advanced Headquarters. — CROISILLES CAVES. T.24.a.9.6.

No. 1 Section. — do do do

No. 3 Section. — do do do

No. 2 Section. — HAMELINCOURT - ready to move at 10 minutes notice.

No. 4 Section. — HAMELINCOURT - ready to move as Mobile Section at 30 minutes notice.

3.   Advanced Company Headquarters will be established at 9.30 p.m. November 19th.

4.   No. 1 Section under organisation already arranged will be in BURG SUPPORT with the wiring Companies of the Assaulting Battalions.   To be in position by 6.30 a.m. "Z" day.

5.   No. 3 Section will be disposed in two parties as follows, to superintend digging of Communication Trenches :-

Left Party under 2nd. Lieut OSMOND in HIND SUPPORT.

Right Party under Sergeant HEWITT in BURG SUPPORT on the Right of the wiring Companies.

6.   No. 2 will be the reserve Section.   Two pontoon wagons will be held ready to carry this Section forward at 10 minutes notice.

7.   No. 4 will be organised as a Mobile Section and must be ready to move quickly and to deal with obstructions, repair bridges and open up water supplies. (Explosives, wire ropes and well buckets, block and tackles, cross cut saws, felling axes and a good supply of spikes and nails are indispensible.)

8.   No. 2 Section will send two Cycle Orderlies to C.R.Es Headquarters, MERCATEL on evening of 19th.

9.   A brief daily report of work done to be sent to
/Advanced

Page 3.

Advanced Company Headquarters by 8.30 a.m. to include work done during night.

10. A copy of what a Section must be prepared to do in the event of it being placed at the disposal of an Infantry Brigade during an Enemy Withdrawal has been sent to each Section Officer.

11. As a later operation, if possible, a second belt of wire will be run along the front of TUNNEL TRENCH from U.7.d.85.10 to DIANA. (length approx. 600 yards).

12. Nos. 1 and 3 Sections will, in the event of the work of wiring and digging Communication Trenches being got through as quickly as anticipated, get into touch with Battalion or Company Commanders in the line and give what assistance they can up to Zero plus 6 hours, when if no other orders have been received and events seem favourable they may withdraw to CROISILLES CAVES.

The earlier a start is made on revetting bad parts of new trenches the better. There is a good preliminary supply in JANET DUMP. No. 1 Section will work in the Right Battalion Area and No. 3 Section in the Left.

13. Dress - skeleton order - full Iron Rations and also a haversack ration, with filled water bottles to be carried.

P. F. Whittall

Major R. E.

O.C. 157th. (Field) Company R. E.

Copy No. 1   O.C. Company.
    2   C. R. E.
    3   2nd. in Command.
    4   O.C. No. 1 Section.
    5   O.C. No. 2 Section.
    6   O.C. No. 3 Section.
    7   O.C. No. 4 Section.
    8   2nd. Lieut. BANCROFT.
   9 & 10   War Diary.

WAR DIARY

FOR MONTH OF DECEMBER, 1917.

VOLUME :- 25.

UNIT :- 157th Field Coy R.E.

CONFIDENTIAL.

WAR DIARY

OF THE

157th. (FIELD) COMPANY R. E.

from 1st. December 1917   to   31st. December 1917.

Army Form C. 2118.

WAR DIARY
of
INTELLIGENCE SUMMARY.
(Erase heading not required.)

December 1917

Place	Date	Hour	Summary of Events and Information	Remarks and references to Appendices
HAMELINCOURT	1st		Company working on Right Sub-section of Left Section of 16th Divisional Front. Nos. 1, 3 & 4 Sections in Advanced Billets and working on the Line. No. 2 Section at Company H.Q. on Intermediate Work. Letter of congratulation to Divisional R.E. received by 16th Divisional Commander.	
	2nd		Work as above.	
	3rd		Work as above.	
	4th		Nos. 1, 3 & 4 Sections returned to Company H.Q. Dismounted portion of Company left HAMELINCOURT by Motor Lorry at 10.0 am and Mounted portion of the Company by road at 9.0 am. Orders previously issued were cancelled on the road and Company was ordered to stay the night at BARASTRE. O.C. remained at HAMELINCOURT to hand over work in Line to O.C. 331st (Field) Coy. R.E.	
	5th	8.30am	10 O.R. joined as reinforcements. Company left BARASTRE under orders of 49th I.B. and move	

Army Form C. 2118.

WAR DIARY
INTELLIGENCE SUMMARY.
(Erase heading not required.)

November 1917.

Place	Date	Hour	Summary of Events and Information	Remarks and references to Appendices
	6th		Sy road to TINCOURT. HAMEL. O.C rejoined the Company	
	7th	11.15am	Orders received from C.R.E. for move	
		11.45am	Company marched off and moved to VILLERS-FAUCON.	
			I. O. R. joined as reinforcements - No 1, 3 + 4 Sections working in LEMPIRE DEFENCES	
	8th		No 2 Section working in Camp	
			Certain parties working at night on construction of a new French system	
	9th		French party in forward system	
			Working relief on new French started. Orders received from C.R.E. re "Standing to" in readiness for enemy attack.	
	10th		No 1 & 3 Sections relieved 2 Sections 155th (Field) Coy R.E. in advanced billets at RONSSOY and work in Left Brigade Area	
	11th 12th		No 4 Section working on new Brigade HQ in QUARRY.	

WAR DIARY
or
INTELLIGENCE SUMMARY.

(Erase heading not required.)

November 1917

Army Form C. 2118.

Place	Date	Hour	Summary of Events and Information	Remarks and references to Appendices
	13		2nd Lt. T.C. GLYNN and 8 O.R. of No. 2 Section moved to Advanced Billets. 2nd Lt. E.N BANCROFT rejoined from leave.	
	14th 15th		Work as above	
	16		Company H.Q. shelled about 9.0 P.M. No casualties in Company. 2 mules wounded — one had to be destroyed.	
	17th		Lieut. J.C. BLACK granted leave to U.K. Company completed its second year in France	
	18th		Work as above.	
	19th		1 O.R. wounded in action	
	20		2nd Lt. T.C. GLYNN and 8 O.R. of No. 2 Section left Advanced Billets and rejoined Company H.Q.	
	21st to 23rd		Work as above.	

Army Form C. 2118.

WAR DIARY
or
INTELLIGENCE SUMMARY.
(Erase heading not required.)

December 1917

Instructions regarding War Diaries and Intelligence Summaries are contained in F. S. Regs., Part II. and the Staff Manual respectively. Title pages will be prepared in manuscript.

Place	Date	Hour	Summary of Events and Information	Remarks and references to Appendices
	24th		No. 1 & 3 Sections returned to Company H.Q. from Advanced Billets.	
	25th		Company assembled at H.Q. to celebrate Christmas Day	
	26th		No. 2 & 4 Sections moved to Advanced Billets. Nos 1 & 3 Sections working on new Brigade H.Q. in QUARRY.	
	27th		Work as above. 1 O.R. 2/8th Manchester Regt joined with view to transfer	
	28th		20 O.R. joined as reinforcements. Company relieved of work on Line Day 156th (Fus) Company R.E.	
	29th		Work as above. 31 O.R. 1/8th Royal Inniskilling Fus. join on attachment	

WAR DIARY
INTELLIGENCE SUMMARY.

(Erase heading not required.)

November 1917.

Army Form C. 2118.

Place	Date	Hour	Summary of Events and Information	Remarks and references to Appendices
CROISILLES HEIGHTS	30th		Military Medal Ribbons presented by C.R.E. to the following N.C.O. and men for good work during the capture of Croisilles Heights. No. 108956 Lance Corp. FURNESS A. 16902 Sapper BARDNER A. 43489 Sapper KAY P.N.	
	31st		Work as above	

P. Whittall
MAJOR, R.E.
O.C. 157th (FIELD) COMPANY R.E.

WD 26

WAR DIARY,

FOR MONTH OF JANUARY, 1918.

VOLUME :- 26.

UNIT :- 157th Fd. Coy. R.E.

WAR DIARY
INTELLIGENCE SUMMARY
(Erase heading not required.)

151st (Field) Co. R.E.

January 1916

Army Form C. 2118.

Place	Date	Hour	Summary of Events and Information	Remarks and references to Appendices
VILLERS FAUCON	1st		Company working in Faucon Area	
	2nd		2.O.R. joined as reinforcements.	
	3rd		Work as above	
	4th		Lieut. J C Black reported from leave.	
	5th		Work as above	
	6th		1.O.R wounded in action	
			2nd Lt J R Osmond granted leave to U.K.	
	7th to 9th		Work as above.	
	10th		2nd Lt J L Glynn attached 156th (Field) Coy R.E.	
			1.O.R joined as reinforcement.	
	11th		Work as above.	
	12th		Company relieved 156th (Field) Coy R.E. in line. Nos 1 & 2	

WAR DIARY
INTELLIGENCE SUMMARY.
(Erase heading not required.)

Army Form C. 2118.

57th (Field) Coy. R.E.

January 1916.

Place	Date	Hour	Summary of Events and Information	Remarks and references to Appendices
	13th		Stations forwarded to advanced Billets in PONSSOY.	
	14th to 16th		1. O.R. joined as reinforcement. Major R.F. Whittall acting C.R.E. Capt J.R. Greenhow took over command of the Company.	
	17th		Work as above	
	18th		4. O.R. joined as reinforcements.	
	19th		Work as above.	
	20th		1. O.R. joined as reinforcement. Work as above.	
	21st		130. R. joined as reinforcements.	
	22nd		Divisional Headquarters moved to TINCOURT. Major R.F. Whittall proceeded with H.Q. R.E.	

Army Form C. 2118.

WAR DIARY
of
INTELLIGENCE SUMMARY.
(Erase heading not required.)

157th (Field) Company, 64 R.E.

January 1918

Place	Date	Hour	Summary of Events and Information	Remarks and references to Appendices
Advanced Billets.	23rd		No 3rd & 4th Sections relieved 1st & 2nd Sections at Advanced Billets. 2nd Lt J R Osmond rejoined from leave	
	24th		Work as above	
	25th		Work as above	
	26th		2/O.R. joined as reinforcements.	
	27th		Work as above.	
	28th		Work as above.	
	29th	8.45pm	Gas Alarm sounded but proved to be a False Alarm	
	30th		Work as above.	
	31st		1 O.R. joined as reinforcement.	

[signature] Capt. R.E.
for O.C. 157th Field Co. R.E.

Stamp: 157TH (FIELD) COMPANY ROYAL ENGINEERS 2 FEB 1918

Vol 27

WAR DIARY.

FOR MONTH OF FEBRUARY, 1918.

VOLUME:- 27.

UNIT:- 157th Field Coy. R.E.

Army Form C. 2118.

WAR DIARY
INTELLIGENCE SUMMARY.
(Erase heading not required.)

February 1918.

Place	Date	Hour	Summary of Events and Information	Remarks and references to Appendices
VILLERS-FAUCON	1st		Company in Duuenal. Leave. Capt. E.K. GREENHOW commanding Company.	
	2nd		O.C. reported from H.Q., R.E.	
	3rd		Routine work.	
	4th			
	5th		O.C. granted leave to U.K.	
	6th		Routine work.	
	7th		1- O.R. joined as reinforcement.	
	8th		Routine work.	
	9th			
	10th		2nd Lieut. T.C. GLYNN transferred to 156th (Field) Coy. R.E. 1- O.R. wounded in action.	
	11th		Routine work.	
	12th		1- O.R. joined as reinforcement.	

Army Form C. 2118.

WAR DIARY
INTELLIGENCE SUMMARY.

(Erase heading not required)

February 1918.

Instructions regarding War Diaries and Intelligence Summaries are contained in F. S. Regs., Part II. and the Staff Manual respectively. Title pages will be prepared in manuscript.

Place	Date	Hour	Summary of Events and Information	Remarks and references to Appendices
	13th		1 Off. and 25 O.R. 2nd Royal Irish Regt. attached for Special Musketry Work.	
	14th		2nd Lieut. G.H. BAXTER granted leave to U.K.	
	15th		Company relieved 126th (Field) Company R.E. (21st Division) in Epéhy Sector. Nos. 3 & 4 Sections and certain Infantry details proceeded to Advanced Billets in EPEHY.	
	16th to 19th		Routine work.	
	20th		O.C. returned from leave and assumed Command.	
	21st		Routine work. 2nd Lieut. G.H. BAXTER authorised to wear the badges of Lieutenant pending Gazette.	
	22nd 23rd		Routine work.	
	24th		1. O.R. joined as reinforcement.	

Army Form C. 2118.

WAR DIARY
of
INTELLIGENCE SUMMARY. February 1918.
(Erase heading not required.)

Instructions regarding War Diaries and Intelligence Summaries are contained in F. S. Regs., Part II. and the Staff Manual respectively. Title pages will be prepared in manuscript.

Place	Date	Hour	Summary of Events and Information	Remarks and references to Appendices
	25th 26th		Routine work.	
	27th		Routine work. Test "ALERT" VILLERS-FAUCON Defence Scheme carried out.	
		4.45 P.M.	Alarm received.	
		5.17 P.M.	Company ready in battle positions and ordered to disembus.	
	28th		Routine work.	

P. Nuttall.
MAJOR, R.E.
O.C. 167th (FIELD) COMPANY R.E.

16th Divisional Engineers

157th FIELD COMPANY R. E.

MARCH 1918

Army Form C. 2118.

WAR DIARY
INTELLIGENCE SUMMARY.
59th (Field) Company R.E.
March 1918

Place	Date	Hour	Summary of Events and Information	Remarks and references to Appendices
VILLERS-FAUCON	1st		Routine work. Company in Left Sector of 16th Divisional Front.	
	2nd		No. 3 & 4 Sections & certain Infantry details attached to Company H.Q. that G.H. BAXTER returned from leave. Company employed on Reserve work. Routine work.	
	3rd to 9th			
	10th		No. 2 Section proceeded, with certain Infantry details to advanced Billets in RONSSOY. Company takes over work in Right Sector. Captain E.K. GREENHOW granted leave to U.K. Routine work.	
	11th to 13th			
	14th, 15th, 16th			
	17th		No. 1 Section relieved No. 2 Section in advanced Billets at RONSSOY.	

Army Form C. 2118.

WAR DIARY
of
INTELLIGENCE SUMMARY.

151st (Field) Company R.E.

March 1918.

(Erase heading not required.)

Place	Date	Hour	Summary of Events and Information	Remarks and references to Appendices
	18th & 19th		Routine work.	
	20th		2 O.R. joined as reinforcements.	
	21st	4.15 a.m.	Intense bombardment by enemy commenced, all men and animals withdrawn W. of VILLERS FAUCON for safety. About mid-day the dismounted portion were brought back, issued with tools, and proceeded to dig posts in defence of VILLERS-FAUCON.	
		4.30 p.m.	No. 1 Section withdrew, fighting a rearguard action from RONSSOY. After dark the dismounted portion were withdrawn to the GREEN LINE, immediately North and East of HAMEL and proceeded to improve this line for defence.	

The Transport was packed and despatched to MARQUAIX.

CASUALTIES. — 2nd Lt. N.C. GORNELL Killed, 2nd Lieut G.H. BAXTER

WAR DIARY
INTELLIGENCE SUMMARY.
(Erase heading not required.)

Army Form C. 2118.

15th Field Coy. R.E.
March 1918

Place	Date	Hour	Summary of Events and Information	Remarks and references to Appendices
HAMEL.	22nd		wounded, 11. O.R. wounded. 1. O.R. wounded (gas). 2. O.R. missing. Transport moved to HAMEL. Many stragglers collected and sent to garrison GREEN LINE. Patrols sent out, found enemy one man returning wounded, the other two being missing. Enemy seen to be massing for an attack. CASUALTIES. 1. O.R. wounded. 2. O.R. missing (believed prisoners)	
	23rd		Finding that both on the right and on the left out troops had been much drawn from the GREEN LINE, the 15th (Field) Company was instructed at dawn and came under the orders of the 48th I.B forming up in a line East of DOINGT. Transport moved via BIRCHES, HERBECOURT to the West of CAPPY. About mid-day, it was discovered that the enemy had	

Army Form C. 2118.

WAR DIARY
INTELLIGENCE SUMMARY.

157th Field Coy. R.E.

March 1918

(Erase heading not required.)

Place	Date	Hour	Summary of Events and Information	Remarks and references to Appendices
			pushed back the troops on our left and also reinforcements were received, so that our right flank was threatened. At this time the 157th Field Company, and the Hampshire Engineers were working in conjunction, and all the other troops having been withdrawn, it was decided to retire on DOINGT. This retirement was carried out in good order, under heavy machine-gun fire. Rearguard parties were left out and subsequently withdrawn, the men showing a steadiness and fine spirit. Touring parties was everywhere provided for a withdrawal at any party (?) Casualties during this withdrawal — 4 O.R. wounded. Company was then ordered to proceed to BIACHES, where it manned a trench in conjunction with the Somme, until the orders of 48th I.B. were received. Late at night HQ orders to withdraw to CAPPY were received.	
CAPPY	24th		The Company marched, rejoining the transport about	

WAR DIARY
INTELLIGENCE SUMMARY

157th Field Company R.E
March 1918

Date	Hour	Summary of Events and Information	Remarks
25th	4.0 am 5.35 pm	Orders received to pack up and stand by. Immediately afterwards, the Company was ordered to proceed to hold and prepare for demolition the bridge head between MERICOURT and ETINEHAM, the mounted portion) being sent to transport lines N.W. of CORBIE. During the night, two bridges were prepared for demolition - one across the River SOMME and one across the SOMME Canal. The dismounted portion leaving at 9 noon over these bridges, moved into MERICOURT.	
26th	9.30 am	Work for defence of PROYART line commenced at earliest moment. The above mentioned bridges were demolished and commenced at earliest moment. This work was interrupted by the enemy and the 3 Field Companies of the Division withdrawn in Divisional Reserve. CASUALTIES:- 1. O.R. wounded. In the evening after dark the Company was sent	

WAR DIARY
INTELLIGENCE SUMMARY

Army Form C. 2118.

157th Field Company R.E.
March 1918

Place	Date	Hour	Summary of Events and Information	Remarks and references to Appendices
MERCOURT	27th		to take up position on the Ridge running South from MORCOURT & organise strong pts and form a line of defence.	
		1.15 pm	Company ordered to march to MERCOURT, to prolong the left flank of the 49th Brigade with a line of posts. N° 3 Companies were disposed & ground about MERCOURT to cover any possible retirement. The N° 3 Companies were disposed of ground about MERCOURT to cover any possible retirement. About 10.0 a.m. G.O.C. 49th Brigade ordered the 158th & 157th Companies to MORCOURT to again organise the line of defence there. This was done and on the retirement of the Infantry an attempt was made to withdraw the Companies to a new rendezvous near LAMOTTE. The Company was attacked by the Enemy on the night flank from the direction of CERISY. They were however quicker off, and a message to inform 148th Brigade, who had been left in MORCOURT of the retirement, was sent	

Army Form C. 2118.

15th Field Company R.E.
March 1918.

WAR DIARY
INTELLIGENCE SUMMARY.
(Erase heading not required.)

Place	Date	Hour	Summary of Events and Information	Remarks and references to Appendices
LAMOTTE	28th		The Company had to be withdrawn under machine-gun and shell fire, it was eventually put into the line behind LAMOTTE, then being held by the force organized under General CAREY. In the early hours the morning orders were received for details the 16th Division to withdraw to HAMEL. Here the Division was reconstituted and the Divisional Engineer Battalion formed under the Command of Major P.J. WHITTALL, D.S.O., R.E., (commanding 156th (Field) Company R.E.) This Battalion came under the Command of the 48th I.B. The Engineer Battalion remained in close support in the Sunken Road S. of HAMEL. CASUALTIES. 1. O.R. Killed. 3 O.R. Wounded.	
HAMEL	29th		The Engineer Battalion garrisoned some pits in support. The Company Bivouacs underwent enemy shelling	

WAR DIARY 157th Field Company R.E.
INTELLIGENCE SUMMARY.
March 1918.

Place	Date	Hour	Summary of Events and Information	Remarks
HAMEL	30.		After a heavy preliminary bombardment, about noon, the enemy attacked. This attack failed, except on one point. The Divisional Engineer Battalion furnished the counter attack with the 157th & 156th Companies, which was immediately successful. The counter attacking party remained as garrison of the front line. CASUALTIES. 1 Officer wounded. 6. O.R wounded.	
HAMEL	31st.		The Divisional Engineer Battalion remained in line with same dispositions as previous day until relieved on the night of the 31st of March / 1st of April. CASUALTIES. 1. O.R wounded.	

P A Mittall
Major R.E.
O C 157th (Field Coy) R.E.

CONFIDENTIAL.

WAR DIARY

OF THE

157th. (FIELD) COMPANY R.E.

from 1st. April 1918 to 30th. April 1918.

Army Form C. 2118.

WAR DIARY 151st (Sieke) Company T.C.
INTELLIGENCE SUMMARY.
(Erase heading not required.)

April 1918.

Instructions regarding War Diaries and Intelligence Summaries are contained in F. S. Regs., Part II. and the Staff Manual respectively. Title pages will be prepared in manuscript.

Place	Date	Hour	Summary of Events and Information	Remarks and references to Appendices
AUBIGNY.	1st 2nd		Routine work.	
	3rd	4.0 am	Company left AUBIGNY and moved from BLANGY-TRONVILLE by Motor Bus to SALEUX. The transport proceeded by road from AUBIGNY to SALEUX.	
SALEUX	4th	9.0 am	Transport left SALEUX and moved by road to ONICOURT arriving here at 5 h.	
		1.30 pm	Dismounted personnel left SALEUX and marched to Railway Station.	
	5th	10 am	Dismounted personnel entrained and moved by rail detraining at BLANGY. The journey was completed by road to ONICOURT.	
ONICOURT	6th to 8th		Routine work.	

Army Form C. 2118.

WAR DIARY
INTELLIGENCE SUMMARY.
(Erase heading not required.)

157th (Field) Company R.E.
April 1918

Instructions regarding War Diaries and Intelligence Summaries are contained in F. S. Regs., Part II. and the Staff Manual respectively. Title pages will be prepared in manuscript.

Place	Date	Hour	Summary of Events and Information	Remarks and references to Appendices
	9th		C.R.E. inspected the Company.	
	10th		Routine work	
	11th			
	12th	3.20 p.m.	Orders received	
		5.45 p.m.	Company moved by road to NOIREL.	
NOIREL.	13th	9.30 a.m.	Company moved by road to FERRIERES.	
	14th		Routine work.	
FERRIERES	15th		Company commenced work on G.H.Q. defence	
	16th		,,	
	17th		Routine work.	

WAR DIARY

157th (Field) Company R.E.

INTELLIGENCE SUMMARY

April 1918

Army Form C. 2118.

Place	Date	Hour	Summary of Events and Information	Remarks and references to Appendices
	18th		Lieut. R.F. OD PEET joined for duty.	
	19th to 27th		Routine work.	
	28th	1.0 pm	Company left Willis and marched to AILLY-SUR-SOMME.	
		6	F.O.R. joined as reinforcement.	
	29th	10.40 pm	Company entrained.	
	30th	10.0 am	Company detrained at THIENNES and marched by road to ISBURGUES.	
		6		
ISBURGUES	30th	10.0 am	Company left ISBURGUES and took over 56th (Field) Company Billets at PEQUER.	
		6	4.2.O.R. joined as reinforcements.	

H.H. Mitchell
MAJOR, R.E.
O.C. 157th (FIELD) COMPANY R.E.

Vol 30

CONFIDENTIAL.

WAR DIARY

OF THE

157th. (FIELD) COMPANY R.E.

from   1st. May 1918   to   31st. May 1918.

Army Form C. 2118.

WAR DIARY MAY 1918
or
INTELLIGENCE SUMMARY. 187 Tellay RE

(Erase heading not required.)

Instructions regarding War Diaries and Intelligence Summaries are contained in F. S. Regs., Part II. and the Staff Manual respectively. Title pages will be prepared in manuscript.

Place	Date	Hour	Summary of Events and Information	Remarks and references to Appendices
PECQUEUR 36A Sheet I.20.b.	1/5/18		Work on G.H.Q. defence line at ISBERGUES. Lt RIDD Reid and No 3 Section working under C.R.E. South. 2Lt C H BOYCE joined for duty. RBJ	
	2/5/18		3 O.R. reinforcements joined. RBJ	
	3/5/18		Major P F WHITTALL DSO RE left Coy. Captain TERJEMANN RE RE took over command. 1SBERGUES RBJ	
	4/5/18		1, 2 and 4 sections work on 3, 4 and 5 sections G.H.Q. line. No 3 section ISBERGUES RBJ	
	5/5/18		Work as above RBJ	
	6/5/18		Work as above. CRE 16th Div held special parade for distribution of M Medal. RBJ	
	7/5/18		Work as above. RBJ	
	8/5/18		Work as above RBJ	
	9/5/18		Work as above RBJ. 1 OR reinforcement joined. RBJ	
	10/5/18		Work as above RBJ	
	11/5/18		Work as above RBJ	
	12/5/18		Work as above RBJ	
	13/5/18		Work as above RBJ	
	14/5/18		Work as above RBJ	

WAR DIARY 157 Field Coy RE
INTELLIGENCE SUMMARY. MAY 1918

Army Form C. 2118.

Place	Date	Hour	Summary of Events and Information	Remarks and references to Appendices
PECQUEUR 36A I.10.b.	15/5/18		Work on FHQ lines as above	RB
	16/5/18		Work as above	RB
	17/5/18		Coy came under administration CRE 14 and Tactical orders of 15th C 40st Inf Bde	RB
	18/5/18		On 16 Div leaving area	RB
	19/5/18		Work on FHQ line as above. Orders for 14th Div defence scheme received	RB
	20/5/18		Work as above. Coy defence scheme issued	RB
	21/5/18		Practice MAN BATTLE STATIONS. Work in afternoon as usual	RB
	22/5/18		Work as usual	RB
	23/5/18		Work as above	RB
	24/5/18		Work in 3, 4 and 5 subsectors GHQ line as usual. 2/Sergt BOOTHROYD RE proceeded to ENGLAND for RE cadet Course	RB
	25/5/18		Work as usual	RB
	26/5/18		Work as above	RB
	27/5/18		Work as above	RB
	28/5/18		Work as above	RB
	29/5/18		Work as above. RB CRE 16 came to see coy. RB CRE 14 and BOURTHES received from CRE 14	RB
	30/5/18		Work as usual. Orders known to COYECQUE and BOURTHES received from CRE 14	RB
COYECQUE	31/5/18		S. M. R. handed over to OC 156 Field Coy, 16 Div. Company marched to COYECQUE arrived 8.0 pm	RB

R.H. Plummer Major
157th Field Coy RE 7/6/18

CONFIDENTIAL.

WAR DIARY

of the

157th. (FIELD) COMPANY R.E.

from 1st. JUNE 1918 to 30th. JUNE 1918.

Army Form C. 2118.

WAR DIARY
or
INTELLIGENCE SUMMARY. 157 Field Coy R.E. JUNE 18

(Erase heading not required.)

Army Form C. 2118.

Instructions regarding War Diaries and Intelligence Summaries are contained in F. S. Regs., Part II. and the Staff Manual respectively. Title pages will be prepared in manuscript.

Place	Date	Hour	Summary of Events and Information	Remarks and references to Appendices
COYECQUE	1st	1.0p.	Left by road for BOURTHES	R/BJ
BOURTHES CALAIS 13.F.5.23	2nd		Arrived BOURTHES F.S.2.3. 5.0pm R/BJ Coy on drill and camp duties R/BJ	
	3rd	8.0 A.m	Lt Mulch and No 4 section to ENQUIN for BAILOW trestlem. staying camp CALAIS 13. E.6.1.9 R/BJ	
	4th	2 pm	2/Lt BANCROFT and No 2 section to SENLECQUES. Calais 13 F.5. 3.7	
		"	Lt PEET and No 3 section to MARQUISE Sheet 13 F.6. 3.5. R/BJ	
		2.pm	Coy HQ and No 1 section to WICQUINGHEM F.6. 50.95 R/BJ	
WICQUINGHEM Calais 13	5th		Section on reconnaissance and work 2/Lt C.H. BOYCE (Monkey Side R/B) 2/Lt BLACK at ENQUIN R/BJ	
	6th		" " " " meanwhile No 1 section went to ENQUIN R/BJ	
	7th.		work as above. R/BJ	
	8th		Move to LACRES except No 4 & No 1 sec attached which remained at ENQUIN. R/BJ	
LACRES Calais 13 D.5.05.15.	9th		Section efficer taking over DOUDEAUVILLE & HALINGHEN areas from 1st KENT R/BJ R/BJ	
	10th		" " " R/BJ	
	11th		No 1 section returned to HQ except detachment left at ENQUIN No 2 to FRENCQ No 3 to PARENTY No 4 to BERNIEULLE. R/BJ	
	12th		Work on reconnaissance & training facilities in DOUDEAUVILLE & HALINGHEN areas R/BJ	
	13th		Work as above R/BJ	
	14th		" " " R/BJ	
	15th		" " " R/BJ	
	16th		" " " R/BJ	

Army Form C. 2118.

WAR DIARY
or
INTELLIGENCE SUMMARY.

(Erase heading not required.)

152 Field Coy RE
JUNE 1918

Instructions regarding War Diaries and Intelligence Summaries are contained in F. S. Regs., Part II. and the Staff Manual respectively. Title pages will be prepared in manuscript.

Place	Date	Hour	Summary of Events and Information	Remarks and references to Appendices
LACRES DS.05.15	17th		Work on DOISEAUVILLE & HALINGHEM areas (Training facilities & accommodation)	RE/
	18th		Work as above RE/	
	19th		Work as above RE/	
	20th		Work as above RE/	
	21st		Work as above RE/	
	22nd		Work as above RE/	
	23rd		Work as above Sent C.O. to RE School HOURQUET as instructor RE/	
	24th		Work as above RE/	
	25th		Work as above RE/	
	26th		Work as above RE/	
	27th		Work as above. 9 O.R. sent to Sect USA Engrs at MENTY as instructors 4 PEET return men work in CAMPAGNE area from 208 Field Coy, ENGINEERS RE/	
	28th		Work as above. Taking over work from 208 Fd Coy RE. 2 OR sent to CATELET to	
	29th		take charge of shops RE/ RE/	
	30th		Work as above. RE/	
			Work as above	

(Sgd) W Fanning Major RE

O C 152 Field Coy RE

3/7/18

CONFIDENTIAL

WAR DIARY

OF THE

157th. (FIELD) COMPANY R. E.

from 1st JULY 1918 to 31st. JULY 1918.

Army Form C. 2118.

WAR DIARY
or
INTELLIGENCE SUMMARY.
(Erase heading not required.)

7/157 Fld Coy RE
JULY 1918

Place	Date	Hour	Summary of Events and Information	Remarks and references to Appendices
LACRES S.D. Column 13	1/7/18		Coy HQ and No 1 Section at LACRES. No 2 at FRENCQ. No 3 PARENTY. No 4 BERNIEULLE. Work on administration & Training Frielties in DRETONNELLS & HALIFATION areas 2/Lt J.BROOM arrived and posted to 3 Section 30/6/18 and took over No 1 Section. RRG	
	2/7/18		Work as above RRG	
	3/7/18		Sent J. LOW mounted from RE Scol/Infantry Schl to HOURQUET RRG	
	4/7/18		Work as above. RE Technical unit 305 Engrs U.S.A. reported coy. RRG	
	5/7/18		Work as above. Bombardments RRG	
	6/7/18		Work as above RRG	
	7/7/18		Sunday Rest day periodical inspection of section RRG	
	8/7/18		Work as above RRG	
	9/7/18		Work as above RRG	
	10/7/18		2/Lt BANCROFT on leave U.K. 2/Lt BROOM + No 1 section return No 2 at FRENCQ RRG 2/Lt ROBERTS joins Coy for duty. No 2 section return to Coy HQ much 2/Lt ROBERTS.	
	11/7/18		Work as above RRG	
	12/7/18		Work as above RRG	
	13/7/18		14 dismounted and 3 mounted reinforcements of vard coy today. hrle on above RRG	
	14/7/18		Rest day from. Reinforcements allotted + sent out to sections RRG	
	15/7/18		Work as above RRG	

Army Form C. 2118.

157 Fld Coy RE
JULY 1918

WAR DIARY
or
INTELLIGENCE SUMMARY.
(Erase heading not required.)

Instructions regarding War Diaries and Intelligence Summaries are contained in F.S. Regs., Part II. and the Staff Manual respectively. Title pages will be prepared in manuscript.

Place	Date	Hour	Summary of Events and Information	Remarks and references to Appendices
LACRES Calais 13. S.D.	16/7/18		Work as above. RBJ.	
	17/7/18		Work as above morning. Wagon & harness cleaning afternoon RBJ	
	18/7/18		Inspection by E-in-C of Coy. at LA VENTE VOIE (LACRES) at 11.0am 2/Lt ROBERTS to BERNEVILLE	
			& Lath grove area and No 4 section from Lt BLACK. RBJ.	
	19/7/18		Lt. BLACK to H.Q.E. RBJ	
	20/7/18		Work as usual. RBJ Very heavy thunderstorm 4 pm R.A.	
	21/7/18		Rest day. Coy went to Sunken pools given by C.R.E. at SAMER RBJ.	
	22/7/18		Work as usual. RBJ.	
	23/7/18		No 3 section return from PARENTY to LACRES leaving 4 detached RBJ	
	24/7/18		No 3 section training (musketry) No 1 section returned from FRANCQ leaving 1 spr detached RBJ	
	25/7/18		Nos 1,2 + 3 training. No 4 work in ANDEAVILLE south AREA. RBJ.	
	26/7/18		Nos 1,2 + 3 musketry. No 4 returned from BERNEVILLE leaving 2 detached. Lt Sumner RE came	
	27/7/18		came this afternoon RBJ. Lt ENSORCROFT from France U.K. RBJ.	
	28/7/18		Nos 1 + 3 firing on BEZINGHEM range. Nos 1 + 4 on Rifle range. RBJ.	
			(Coy tournament on BEZINGHEM range. No 4 section wins. RBJ.	
HARDELOT PLAGE Calais 13.	29/7/18		Coy moved to HARDELOT PLAGE (Calais 13) 8.0 am RBJ.	
	30/7/18		Baggage (&) men & transport morning at HARDELOT. Practice build on strand Swimming afternoon CRE came to pontoon ground RBJ.	
	31/7/18		Training as above. Myes pontooning 9 - 4.45 pm RBJ.	

[signature] Lt 7/Fld Coy RE 31/7/18

WAR DIARY

OF THE

157th. (FIELD) COMPANY R. E.

from 1st. August 1918 to 31st. August 1918.

Army Form C. 2118.

WAR DIARY
or
INTELLIGENCE SUMMARY.
(Erase heading not required.)

157 Fld Coy RE   August 1918

Place	Date	Hour	Summary of Events and Information	Remarks and references to Appendices
HARDELOT PLACE Calm 13.5A	1		In bivouac till midday. SyGG on strand in afternoon 8109. H ENBANCRNT and on to FRENCQ to arrange billets RB9.	
FRENCQ Calm 13 (6C Sp.72)	2		March to FRENCQ 1pm. arrived 5pm RB9	
	3		Coy on billet improvements RB9.	
	4		Half day. Coy E service at LETONE 11.30am RB9	
	5		Coy on training and allotments to facilities of HALINGHEN over RB9	
	6		Work as above RB9	
	7		Work as above. My CRE inspected transport 3.30pm RB9.	
	8		Work as above RB9	
	9		Started on CRE programme of training. CRE inspected ammunition and footballs. Work as above RB9	
	10			
	11		Rest day. Coy E + R.C. services RB9	
	12		Work as above RB9 RB9	
	13		Work as above	
	14		Work as above 5 reinforcements joined today RB9.	
	15		Work as above RB9	
	16		Work as above. Wiring demonstrated at HALINGHEN + HONFRIENT OC went to CRE Conference 2.30pm SOMER RB9.	

Army Form C. 2118.

WAR DIARY
or
INTELLIGENCE SUMMARY. 157 Fld Coy RE
(Erase heading not required.)

AUGUST 1918

Instructions regarding War Diaries and Intelligence Summaries are contained in F.S. Regs., Part II. and the Staff Manual respectively. Title pages will be prepared in manuscript.

Place	Date	Hour	Summary of Events and Information	Remarks and references to Appendices
HENCQ Column 13 6C39.79	17/8/18		Work as above. No. 4 Bers + dept. Miller E 1st Corps Ine. school. 1 FEET & MARENTRY 6.7pm 47 1st above Martin. RBJ	
	18/8/18		Cleaning and Mailing transport. 1 FEET to MOEUX LES MINES RBJ	
BAJUS LENS II F.I.	19/8/18		Transport + cyclist to QUENT under Captn Seanham w 2 409 Fd Coy RE at ANNEQUIN RBJ	
	20/8/18		Coy dismounted move to DIEVAL area by bus. Billets at BAJUS. Transport moved on from 409 Fd Coy RE at ANNEQUIN RBJ	
SAILLY LABOURSE	21/8/18		Coy dismounted from DIEVAL & BAJUS by bus marched from BAJUS to SAILLY LABOURSE where billeted for night. Transport moved from BRUAY ANVIN to MAISNIL & RUITZ RBJ	
ANNEQUIN F23 Central	22/8/18		Coy moved to ANNEQUIN into billets of 409 Fd Coy RE. OC took over work from OC 409. Transport remained in lorries at MAISNIL & RUITZ RBJ	
	23/8/18		Work in line below and on pillars. No 3 section left Battn No 2 Cycl Battn area No 1 RBJ	
			CAMBRIN defences No 4 Supplementary above and HQ RBJ	
	24/8/18		Work as above. Some Blue x gas shelling 10pm + 2am RBJ	
	25/8/18		Work as above RBJ	
	26/8/18		Work as above RBJ	
	27/8/18		Work as above. Lt GALLAGHER 1st Fd Coy RE attached for duty. P-te Po CAMBRIN defence with No Section RBJ	
	28/8/18		Work as above RBJ	
	29/8/18		Work as above. No enemy mine but with Coy + 5.1 Bde RBJ	
	30/8/18		Work as above RBJ	
	31/8/18		2Lt ROBERTS + 2 Lt MERCER returned from 1st Corps Gas School + remained with CRE RBJ	

RB Jennings
Major R.E.
O.C. 157th (Field) Company R.E. 31/8/18

WAR DIARY

OF THE

157th. (FIELD) COMPANY R.E.

from 1st. September 1918 to 30th. September 1918.

Army Form C. 2118.

WAR DIARY
or
INTELLIGENCE SUMMARY.
(Erase heading not required.)

Instructions regarding War Diaries and Intelligence Summaries are contained in F. S. Regs., Part II. and the Staff Manual respectively. Title pages will be prepared in manuscript.

Place	Date	Hour	Summary of Events and Information	Remarks and references to Appendices
ANNEQUIN Fd Cent	1/9/18		No 3 section from our left. No 2 from on right. No 1 in Cambrin defences. Yesterday attached from 1st Welsh MGB returned to unit. No 4 in Cambrin defences. Fly RE sand bin. RBY.	
	2/9/18		No working parties owing to heavy bombardment in preparation for the attack at disposal of Brigade. Two sections + two officers at disposal of Brigade.	
	3/9/18		No 4 section taken over from No 3 in afternoon. MGY. No 4 works for and left. No 3 in Cambrin defences. No. 3 section detailed by RBY.	
	4/9/18		One complete section attached to Bde. No 3 section detailed by RBY.	
	5/9/18		No 3 at disposal of MBde. No 2 right fwd and No 1 Cambrin defences. No 4 left forward. MBY.	
	6/9/18		Two sections at disposal of Bde. Nos 3+4. No 1 worked left forward. No 2 right forward.	
	7/9/18		No 3 section consolidation near Spotted Dog. No 4 consolidation AUBURN Trench. No 2 in forward C.Ts. No 1 in old frontline left.	

Army Form C. 2118.

WAR DIARY
or
INTELLIGENCE SUMMARY.
(Erase heading not required.)

Instructions regarding War Diaries and Intelligence Summaries are contained in F. S. Regs., Part II. and the Staff Manual respectively. Title pages will be prepared in manuscript.

Place	Date	Hour	Summary of Events and Information	Remarks and references to Appendices
ANNEQUIN Pisdret	8/9/18		No 3 m forward tracks left front. No 4 camp in concentration AUBURN. Wind abt 3 gas. Ipswich sap & Brown iron forward CTs. No 1 m rear with No 2 m forward CTs Tk lane. All four section m rear with No 2 m forward CTs Tk lane. war plous atchipound of Bde from worn tottery.	
	9/9/18		All 4 section under projecte. No 2 continuing 16 Gun CT. No 1 tracking B.W. concretions. No 3 m forward tracks left front. No. m forward CTs Ipswich sap & Woodadsap. wrt.	
	10/9/18		From 10.0. am today 2 sections only occupied Morgaib. Nos 1 and 4 utthalis. No 1 Cleard Kaburske road of wini and duds. No 3 m extension of Tramway KDA No 4 working for Right Battn m forward CTs No 2 Cleaning track front line gunur.	
	11/9/18		No 1 section m forward track Left Battn No 2 43 m Tramways. No 3 m forward CTs Right Battn.	

D. D. & L., London, E.C.
(A8049) Wt W17771/M2958 750,000 5/17 Sch. 53 Forms/C2118/14

Army Form C. 2118.

WAR DIARY
or
INTELLIGENCE SUMMARY.
(Erase heading not required.)

Instructions regarding War Diaries and Intelligence Summaries are contained in F. S. Regs., Part II. and the Staff Manual respectively. Title pages will be prepared in manuscript.

Place	Date	Hour	Summary of Events and Information	Remarks and references to Appendices
ANNEQUIN	12/9/18		Sections worked in consolidating Rly tramways work. 1st POST. No 2 & 3 on tramways. No 1 on consolidation of new reported post. MSJ	
Posthurt	13/9/18		No 1 section consolidated Rly D in A23a and No 4 carried stores to Railway Cottage. Nos 2 & 3 on tramways. MSJ	
	14/9/18		No 1. men were used for consolidation & to reconnoitre and interpose the area and set the repair in readiness to Reserve Line. No 4 cleared & restored spoil in CEMETERY ALLEY. No 2 & 3 on tramway relaid. MSJ	
	15/9/18		No 1 section unloading left hip Posth cleared the Canal Towpath. No 4 consolidated and wired apart support AUCHY easterly. No 2 on tramway. No 5 on pioneers work in CWINCHY and withdrawing trench lines change from bridge in LA BASSÉE road. MSJ	
	16/9/18		No 3 as above. No 1 as above. No 2 as above No 1 consolidated Newport in AZMUTH alley. Trench ADR on line GAUCHY. MSJ	
	17/9/18		Nos 3 and 2 as above No 1 consolidated Newport in AZMUTH alley. No 4 consolidated On right or AUCHY alley. MSJ	

D. D. & L., London, E.C.
(A8609) Wt W7771/M8031 750,000 5/17 **Sch. 52** Forms/C2118/14

Army Form C. 2118.

WAR DIARY
or
INTELLIGENCE SUMMARY. 1ST/7TH Coy M.O. SEPTEMBER 1918

(Erase heading not required.)

Instructions regarding War Diaries and Intelligence Summaries are contained in F. S. Regs., Part II. and the Staff Manual respectively. Title pages will be prepared in manuscript.

Place	Date	Hour	Summary of Events and Information	Remarks and references to Appendices
ANNEQUIN F.2.3.dist	18/9/18		All weeks duties & Repair Watson at called for. Nos 2 and 3 on alm host. Excavating instructional in Rys bth front. M89.	
	19/9/18		No 1. Wiring the front in VERTALLEY. No @ 2 on alm. cumulating Railway trough No54 as above. The 2nd situation.	
	20/9/18		Nos 1 and 3 on cumulating Railway through No54. Capt Green hum stopped M89. Coys in AUCHY and as above. Mj. R.2 on training hrs	
	21/9/18		No 3 headed over Railway through 6 to 5th Division The Coy H.O. No 1 and 2 on training. No 4 as above. RE)	
	22/9/18		No 4 wrked in jurisdiction in Rysait area. Nos 1 & 2 on training. No 3. In camp. Totals were markd at 1 Knots to form 15th Dukes. 9 handed our Support & codes to Lt PEET. R.E. Handed over tramway to 156 Indry 116 RE)	
	23/9/18		Major JENNINGS. M.C. R.E. Arranged an leave. Company relieved 156 Machine 152 Date over their billets at SAILLY-LA-BOURSE. Horse lines Moved to K 3d 5.7. A4B. 20.00. Lt BLACK. R.E. returned. Coy form H.Q.R.S. 16 O.R.s & Handed to hvrse lines at DROUVIN au DRAIEPORT Major [signature]	

D. D. & L. London, E.C. (A3001) W. W 7777/M3011 750,000 5/17 Sch. 32 Forms/C2118/14

WAR DIARY
or
INTELLIGENCE SUMMARY

Army Form C. 2118.

15th Field Coy R.E.

SEPTEMBER

Place	Date	Hour	Summary of Events and Information	Remarks and references to Appendices
SAILLY-LABOURSE L.3.a.3.8.	22/9/18		Started ½ section holiday. No 1 Section working on repair to Div. H.Q. fillets. No 2 Section erecting sheds at refilling point HOUCHIN, for Div. Train. No 3 Section metalling Route 10 - no working party turned up - bad weather. No 2 section fixing gas proof curtains to cellars in ANNEQUIN, for Res. Batts.	
	23/9/18		No 1 section repairs to Div. H.Q. fillets. No 2 erection shed at refilling point HOUCHIN for Div. Train. ½ No 3 section at HORSE LINES (DROUVIN-K 3d 5.7) making concrete stores. Other half metalling Route 10 (A20a). No 2 section fixing gas proof curtains to billets in ANNEQUIN for sections of 2 English shelters at F9c.2.8 No 1 & 2 section transported to Site of works by 20 motor lorries Adj. G.H.Q. whole ½ supply lorry. Have allotment of present appears on	
	24/9/18		Same as yesterday.	
	27/9/18		Same as yesterday.	
	28/9/18		Work by sections same as 25th, 26th, 27th. No 1 section dismantled Nissen hut in VAUDRICOURT WOOD in chateau grounds (K 3d) to erection at Div. H.Q.	
	29/9/18		No 1 section same as yesterday. No 2 section completed the three refilling point-sheds at HOUCHIN. No 3 ½ sections same as yesterday.	

WAR DIARY

INTELLIGENCE SUMMARY

15th Field Coy R.E. SEPTEMBER

Army Form C. 2118.

Place	Date	Hour	Summary of Events and Information	Remarks and references to Appendices
SAILLY-LABOURSE	30/9/18		No 1 section continued work at Div. H.Q. - same as last six days. No 2 section erecting three Nissen Bow huts at DROUVIN (H.4.C.) for camp accommodation. No 3 section worked as on previous days on installing Route 10 (A 20 a), staking of Company horse lines. No 2 section completed the erection of two complete Hyplus shelters at F 29 c. 9. b. for "B" Coy 16th M.G. ...	

O/C. 15th (FIELD) COMPANY R.E.

Army Form C. 2118.

WAR DIARY / INTELLIGENCE SUMMARY

(Erase heading not required.)

157th Field Co R.E.

OCTOBER

Place	Date	Hour	Summary of Events and Information	Remarks and references to Appendices
SAILLY-LABOURSE. L.3.a.38.	1/10/18		No 3 section working at Anv. H.Q. erecting Nissen Bow hut & two additions to hutts. No 2 section erecting Nissen Bow hut at DROUVIN (K19.a.8.9.), also 3 Sappers enlarging dugout canteen. No 3 section hut being rebuilt route 10 (A7.0.a.) & erecting Tables at Company Horse lines (K.3.d.5.7.) No 4 section erecting English shelter at F.29.c.9.0. for "B" Coy. 16th M.G.	
	2/10/18		Same as yesterday with additional Nissen huts being erected at HOUCHIN for 142nd & 174th (105 A.S.C.) by No 2 section. No 1 section started on our Rover dug out at HAIRPIN DUMP (E.30.a.6.9.)	
	3/10/18		Same as yesterday, with except that No 4 section brought Reconnaissance Wm. S.O. working directly under Lincoln Corps main supply officer as forward at ANNEQUIN (F.23.d.a.n.t.) Eight Sappers No 1 section accompanied by 156 & 5 R.E. Recreation Bridge on VERMELLES - AUCHY Rd. erecting hand railings	
	4/10/18		No 1,2 & 3 sections handing by for emergency whilst in forward area Nine Sappers No 2 section working on erecting Nissen Bow hut at DROUVIN (K.19.a.5.9.) Took an Nissen Bow hut to HOUCHIN Company transport moved up to SAILLY LABOURSE (F.27.d.7.7.) This being then moved to ANNEQUIN took over billet from	
ANNEQUIN F.23.d.94	5/10/18		155th Field Coys. worse flavourings at F.23.d.95. No 1,2,3 sections thunder by for Austrian traversing HAUTE DEULE CANAL, C.13.c, Aug. H.Y. (F.23.d.) No 4 section making recommisance of railways east of railways kindred Corps. water supply officer who making recommisance of directly	

WAR DIARY
INTELLIGENCE SUMMARY

157th Field Coy RE

OCTOBER

Place	Date	Hour	Summary of Events and Information	Remarks and references to Appendices
ANNEQUIN F.23.d.9.4	6/10/18		1/2 No 1 section warning enemy dugouts (in day) action Pays; & reconnoitre standing by for standing to. HAUTE DEULE CANAL. No 2 Section standing by for forward trips. HAUTE DEULE CANAL No 3 Section improving conditions now. Sanitary & making notice boards. No 4 Section on oddwell & working dirty end UP.S. to S.D. (1st BANCROFT) making reconnaissance of railways east of AUCHY (A.23.d)	
AUCHY A.23.d.1.3.	7/10/18		Relieved 155th Field Coy RE at AUCHY & took over, any all ranks, horseline to Henwise Company billeted in old w.d. at A.23.d. No 2 Section improving & making read. Base RO. AUCHY. RHQ & Company makes up of kit HQ & Company fatigues. R.H.Q. Move Divn. records at ANNEQUIN & No 2 Section that & tidy up of equipment & Bdy HQ. AUCHY forwarded all Company fatigues & as certain duty but & ship H.O. & Officers & Battn at BERCLAV (B.19.c). Pair 2 No 1 Sect for sentries at at VERLIN & ELLEU at 8 am I.H.Q.- BILLY-BERCLAU (B.22.cent). NCO. NSenthy. Officer 150 Bdi RHQ. Reconnoitring & making 11 party etc 2 reconnoitre. No 3 section, making location & dispositions of locations of salvage & RE material. Coy Drily fatigues - two men from each section at H.Q. to make reconnaissance of forward area.	
	8/10/18		Nos 1 & 2 Section same as yesterday No 3 Section making location Various frontesides; small party out to wire for trees clearing HAUTE DEULE CANAL. Salvage of RE material. Nosh Jennings Major RE, Thorne time UAM.	

WAR DIARY
or
INTELLIGENCE SUMMARY.

Army Form C. 2118.

(Erase heading not required.)

Place	Date	Hour	Summary of Events and Information	Remarks and references to Appendices
AvcHY Ausd 1.3	10/9/18		1st March R.E. & Corps Troops this morning. No 1 section on BETEN H.Q. No 2 on Bu. H.Q. No 3 Salvage & 2 crew asleep. Base in Walestrope. K.R.J.	
	11/10/18		No 1 on Bn. Hn. H.Q. Billy. No 2 in/out of Tunnels across Bassée Canal Cartwright C.I. B.I.G.b.45.60 No 3 in damning leak at C.17.c.38 No 4 in 6 Suppl. K.R.J.	
	12/10/18		No 1 in led on new billets in HAISNES. +O.P. in BIGY BENEAU. No 2 on Bn.H.Q. & assisting in patrol across HAUTSEDEBULE canal. No 3 in salvage and stopping leak at canal lock C.17.c.3.8. Base on W. Suppl. K.R.J.	
	13/10/18		No 1 recces on new billets in HAISNES. No 2 in Bn.H.Q. No 3 in canal Spurs forward & Dunnington lifting & stopping leak. Was unsuccessful. No 4 in Walestrope. K.R.J.	
	14/10/18		No 1 and 4 as above. No 2 stopped the leak in canal lock tonight. In came in billets except No 3 in Salvage. R&POET	
	15/10/18		Weston Cannon Lottery. Captain SHIRLEY M.C. H.O. 1pm. 1st Field Coy NLS to late on command. WRJ. No 1 as usual in morning. No 2 section put up protective wire on road DEVLSTACT at La PLONES by 3.45p.m. No 2 putting up wire extents Dynamite Factory clearing by 5:30 p.m. No 3 sketch of wire & B11.4 & B20.30 km. No 4 on Walestrope.	

Army Form C. 2118.

WAR DIARY
or
INTELLIGENCE SUMMARY.
(Erase heading not required.)

Title pages OCTOBER 1918   157 Fld Coy RE

Place	Date.	Hour	Summary of Events and Information	Remarks and references to Appendices
BILLY-BERCLAU	16/10/18		Lieut Austin S.O. arr. from BILLY + lifted Transport arrived from unit Lt WOOWARD BE BILLY-at 8 at 10.08am. No 3 Boy sections piled mini craters in main road from Drocourt line through BAUVIN to PROVIN. Ho 1 section tent abeard at ANNOEULIN met Brigade. (47) Cov Hd and Transport moved to BAUVIN. 5pm 23rd Section rejoined from BAUVIN. No 2 section arrived in unit supper in ANNOEULIN No 3 and No 1 section unled in pulling mine craters in ANNOEULIN No 4 at reconnaissance of both RE dumps in PROVIN + in hills No 2 on keep bridging across DEULE under 156 Fld Coy RE No 2 in the STEEPLE.	
BAUVIN	17/10/18	4.0 pm	Transport moved into BAUVIN at 9.0 am the evening M.T.	
	18 ct	0001	Orders recd for Coy to join 47th Bde group at CAMPHIN at 0500. Coy Coff BAUVIN at 0200 and arrived CAMPHIN at 0445. At 0600 recd Secti moved. No 1 + 2 joined N. Advanced Guard + No 3 joined S. Adv. Guard of 47th Bde. Coy HQ + transport moved with main body at 08.30. 47th Bde group in Fd 157 Cy Australia as above marched as vanguard of 16th Div via PHALIMPHIN, ATTICHIES to Point A MARCQ. Sections with advanced guards assisted in passage of Transport road craters which every road blown main roads and removed landmines from streets of PONT A MARCQ, AVELIN and ENNEVELIN. No 1 + 2 Sects arrived at	

Army Form C. 2118.

WAR DIARY
or
INTELLIGENCE SUMMARY.
(Erase heading not required.)

OCTO-DEC 1918

157 FID COY R.E.

Place	Date	Hour	Summary of Events and Information	Remarks and references to Appendices
PONT-A-MARCQ	18th		ENNEVELIN at 1900 and billeted. 3rd & 4th Sects billeted with Coy HQ. at POINT-A-MARCQ.	P
"	19th	8.00	No. 2 Sect rejoined Coy HQ. at Pont-a-MARCQ. Advance continued. No. 1 Sect with N advd Guard, No. 3 Sect with S advd Guard to bridge near MOULIN D'EAU of regimord. Bridges found intact. Sections cleared of obstacles, & moved CORBIEUX and billeted. Coy HQ. and No. 2 Sect moved to TEMPLEUVE at 1560 and billeted. No. 4 Sect remained at PONT-A-MARCQ clearing the town of road mines. Town completely cleared at 1700. No. 4 Sect rejoined Coy at 18.30.	P
TEMPLEUVE	20th		Advance continued. One Sect (No.1) moved with advanced guard from CORBIEUX to RUMES. No. 3 Sect remained at CORBIEUX. Coy HQ. moved with main body at 0845 to CORBIEUX & billeted with No. 3 Sect. Coy HQ. & No 3 Sect moved at 1800 to SENTIÈRE and billeted. No. 2 & 4 Sects moved to RUMES at 1600 & worked with No. 1 Sect on main road to TOURNAI making deviation for transport round a large crater.	P
"	21st		No. 1 & 4 Sections moved at 0800 with advanced guard to a position 1000 yds E.B. TAINTIGNIES and worked on forward roads making them fit for 10-tons transport. Coy HQ. & No 2 Sect moved to TAINTIGNIES north their body at 1100 and billeted. No. 3 Sect worked (with 477 T.M. Batty) on crater on forward road to TOURNAI Road. Job completed at 1800 & No. 3 rejoined Coy HQ. at 1930 and billeted.	P

WAR DIARY
or
INTELLIGENCE SUMMARY.

(Erase heading not required.)

Army Form C. 2118.

Place	Date	Hour	Summary of Events and Information	Remarks and references to Appendices
TAINTIGNIES	22nd	0500	Party 3 R.E. (2 Lt BROOM and 3 N.C.O's/3 Sect) and forward [illeg] to reach to river SCHELDT to recconntr bridges etc. Party accompanied by Infantry Patrol moved forward 1000 yds but came under heavy M.G. and arty fire. Further advance was attempted but forward impossible. Party returned to signed Coy H.Q. 2nd Lt. Sect. started on forward roads. Preparations made for throwing foot-bridges over River SCHELDT at ANTOING in case of further advance. 130 barrels and timber requisitioned for same & required at TAINTIGNIES. Prepared in readiness for use if required.	
do	23rd		Coy remained at TAINTIGNIES. One section & 200 Infantry employed on opening up forward road. One section in camp. Party sent up forward for recce and refs. One section detailed to throw foot-bridge across river SCHELDT at BRUYELLE. No section brought bridges & rafts up to MERLIN but owing to enemy's shell infantry return approaching. W. Lank & Offr party in was abandoned. Bridges dumped at MEZ. VELAIN'S section returned to billets having had 2 men wounded. One Officer made road reconnaissance. One section worked on forward roads until 100 Infy. & many sections	
do	24th 25th		noted. Enemy shelled & none inspected. Major Overgenannt on leave to U.K. Lt. Return Standing by for work in Brigade. An attempt to take further forward Bridges was partially [illeg] owing to enemy [illeg] to evacuation to 2 Brown 2 Horses. Two 3rd Section made out TAINTIGNIES – GUIGNIES Road	
do	26th		Two 1-2 2nd Section worked in Road in yesterday, 2nd in afternoon made the road – do 3rd Section tore up Railway Tracks of BRUYELLE	

D. D. & L., London, E.C.
Wt. W.1771/M.781 750,000 5/17 Sch. 52 Forms/C.2118/14.
(A802a)

Army Form C. 2118.

WAR DIARY
or
INTELLIGENCE SUMMARY.
(Erase heading not required.)

Instructions regarding War Diaries and Intelligence Summaries are contained in F. S. Regs., Part II. and the Staff Manual respectively. Title pages will be prepared in manuscript.

Place	Date	Hour	Summary of Events and Information	Remarks and references to Appendices
TRINTIGNIES	Oct 27		No 3 Section carried up upon Bridging Stone to outskirts of BRUYELLE	
do	28		No 1-2-3-4 Sections on Road as above	
do	29		No 1-2-3-4 Sections on Road as above — Several carts of Bridging going about in Coy. chiefly No 1 - 4 dismounted sections	
do	30		No 1-2 Works on Road as above in morning — No 3 going for material at B.7.C. (Brenen Phillips) not working. Build Wire entanglements No 1 + 2 making Build Wire entanglements. Afternoon for found line running	
do	31st		No 1 + 2 Sections making Shelters & circulation for Front line which were taken up & circulation taken up evening before were checked out in front of trench 14/15 — No 3 Section worked on digging pits defences of ST MAUD - No 4 Section Post defences covering of main line of trenches.	

F. Bowers
Lieut: R.B.
O.O. 157th (Field) Coy. R.E.

Army Form C. 2118.

WAR DIARY or INTELLIGENCE SUMMARY

(Erase heading not required.)

157 Field Coy RE

NOVEMBER 1918

Place	Date Nov	Hour	Summary of Events and Information	Remarks and references to Appendices
TAINTIGNIES (V.26.c - Sheet 37)	1/11/18		Nos 1 & 2 sections Sao cutting [illegible] in front line system (V.19.a 6.rd). No 4 Sect Main line of resistance in LONGUE SAUTE. No 3 section wiring posts in front line system (V.19.a 6.rd). No 4 Sect Main line of resistance in LONGUE SAUTE.	
LA POSTERIE (A.6.c - Sheet 44)	2/11/18		Relieved by 155 Fd Coy R.E. at LA POSTERIE, & took over work in forward area. took over K.OENECK from 156 Fd Coy R.E. About 100 civilian labour working on roads, & 60 infantry.	
	3/11/18		Nos 1 & 3 sections making ferry boats. infantry party to help 2 span R. floating piers at TEMPLEUVE DUMP (F.19.c - Sheet App.) Nos 2 & 4 Sections working on roads.	
	4/11/18		Nos 1, 3 & 4 sections same as yesterday. No 2 section erecting stage etc for DIVISION HQ THEATRE at TEMPLEUVE. T. BANCROFT with Company transport, broke up at night to bridging dump at BRUYELLES (V.26.c.4.2). ferry boats, floating piers & infantry foot bridges; on return [illegible] one driver & two mules wounded.	
	5/11/18		Nos 1 & 3 sections as yesterday. No 2 section at TEMPLEUVE THEATRE at TEMPLEUVE. No 4 section on roads. Floating piers sent forward by company transport, to BRUYELLES bridging dump.	
	6/11/18		Same as yesterday.	
	7/11/18		Nos 1, 2 & 3 sections same as yesterday. No 4 section with 60 infantry salvage of enemy DECAUVILLE track at TEMPLEUVE; also supervision of civilian labour on roads.	

Army Form C. 2118.

WAR DIARY
or
INTELLIGENCE SUMMARY

(Erase heading not required.)

157 FLD COY. R.E.

NOVEMBER — 1918

Place	Date	Hour	Summary of Events and Information	Remarks and references to Appendices
FLORENT (U25a - Sh.t-37)	8/11/18		Company complete with transport moved to FLORENT. No 2 r3 sections (2/Lt IVAN & Lt NORCOMBE) moved forward to BRUYELLES bridging during the evening to the Supplies Pulling floating Infantry Bridges across the Escaut River after the Infantry Patrols had captured the earlier bank. Nos 1+4 Section in reserve.	
ANTOING (V15d - Sh.t-37)	9/11/18		Enemy retired from western bank of Escaut about midnight and was followed up by Infantry Patrols. 2/Lt NORCOMBE with Nos 2 r3 sections for bridged the Escaut with 1 floating bridge at V15c a6 & V15d a8 shortly information of which was obtained from left batt. Company with transport moved forward to ANTOING. No 10 7 sections solving heavy bridging material in rdn to triangle demolished arch bridge, enveloping 26' span — at V15d 3.2.	
	10/11/18		Company moved into allotted billets — CHATEAU in V15b — ANTOING. Nos 1, 2, 3 r4 sections bridging two spans 28', at V15d 32. & V15d 52. for 17 Ton axle load — two Italian PLANTS Proneers assisting.	
	11/11/18		Same as yesterday.	
	12/11/18		Same as yesterday.	
	13/11/18		Same as yesterday.	

WAR DIARY
INTELLIGENCE SUMMARY

Army Form C. 2118.

157 FLD COY R.E.

(Erase heading not required.) — NOVEMBER 1918

Place	Date	Hour	Summary of Events and Information	Remarks and references to Appendices
ANTOING U.25.a — (Sheet 37)	14/11/18		Nos 1, 2, & 3 bridging for 17 tan axle load, details & farm on 14/11/18. No 4 Section covering hurdle & hessian bridge erected by 15 fld Coy. R.E. at V.15.c.22. All material except decking for bridge at V.15.d.32 Salves. Major SHELLY M.C. returned from leave. JR.	SHEET 44.
do	15/11/18		Coy left ANTOING at 11.30 hrs under orders from H.Q. 58 Div. and marched to PONT A RUMES arriving at 14.30 hrs Billeted. JR	SHEET 44.
Pt RUMES	16/11/18		Coy left Pt RUMES at 12.30 hrs marched to PLACE COMPTE arriving at 15.30 hrs. (Under fire order and billeted.) JR	SHEETS 44 and 36A.
Pt RUMES & PLACE COMPTE				
PLACE COMPTE	17/11/18		Coy left PLACE COMPTE at 08.30 hrs and marched to RUE DE MONCHAUX arriving at 13.30 hrs and billeted. Coy came under orders of 7 R.E. 18 Division. 1st Brown returned from leave. JR	do
RUE de MONCHAUX	18/11/18		Coy engaged in arranging billets, cleaning equipment, wagons &c. JR	
do	19/11/18		C.R.E. inspected men of Coy. Remainder of day devoted to cleaning of Coy. billets.	
do	20/11/18		In absence of Coy. Staff parades. Cleaning & working on billets. Preliminary detail	

Army Form C. 2118.

WAR DIARY
INTELLIGENCE SUMMARY.

157 FLD COY R.E.

NOVEMBER 1918

Place	Date	Hour	Summary of Events and Information	Remarks and references to Appendices
Rue de MONCHEVA	21/11/18		of Educational scheme arranged. Sports & Recreation committee formed. Coy. settled in old German huts at LESTREZ. Roll/Parade held. Cleaning up continued.	
do	22/11/18		Roll & Inspection Parade held. Cleaning up continued. Construction of fittings recreation room, reading room, canteen begun. 10 men sent to work. Huts.	
do	23/11/18		Coy. for 22nd D. No 3 section moved to billet in BERSÉE & arranged to work for 49th Inf. Bde.	
do	24/11/18		No 3 section worked with 49th Inf Bde on huttings. Remainder of Coy.	
do	25/11/18		As for 22nd D.	
do	26/11/18		do for 22nd do	
do	27/11/18		do for 22nd D.	
do	28/11/18		Clerk & 3 sappers moved to ATTICHES. Company formed at 12.00 hrs. and billeted P. No 3 Sect. continued work for 49th Inf. Bde. Work on Brigade Theatre at MONS-EN-PEVELE arranged for. One Section worked on RE workshops at ATTICHES. Remainder of Coy on campwork.	
do	29/11/18		One section on H.A.G. Sets. One section levelling stage of MONS-EN-PEVELE Theatre. One section on workshop job. One sect. on RTA in building stables & H.Q. in making tables	
do	30/11/18			

Sheehy Major
O.C. 157 Fd Coy R.E. 1/12/18

War Diary

of the

— 157th (Field) Company R.E. —

From 1st December 1918 to 31st December 1918.

Army Form C. 2118.

WAR DIARY
of
INTELLIGENCE SUMMARY.

(Erase heading not required.)

DECEMBER 1918   151 FIELD Coy R.E.

Instructions regarding War Diaries and Intelligence Summaries are contained in F. S. Regs., Part II. and the Staff Manual respectively. Title pages will be prepared in manuscript.

Place	Date	Hour	Summary of Events and Information	Remarks and references to Appendices
ATTICHES	1/12/18		Connected & placed same Jo.	
do	2/12/18		2 Sections worked with Hq 49th/NF BDE. One Section on workshops.	
"	3rd		One Section assist RFA building stables etc Jo	
"	4/12		As for 2nd Jo	
"	5th		As for 2nd Jo	
"	6th		As for 2nd Jo Jo	
"			No 1 Sect and 3 Sects moved to LUBIARIE near THUMIERES to build, to work on stables for RFA. One Section in Div. Workshops. One Section working for 49th/NF BDE Jo.	
"	7/12		Two 1st 3 Sections working with 16th D.A. No 2 Section in Div. Workshops. No 4 Sect worked for 49th Bde in workshops & on Bg table G. Jo	
"	8th		As noted & placed same Jo	
"	9th		As for 7th Jo Jo	
"	10th		As for 7th Jo Jo	
"	11th		As for 7th Jo Jo	
"	12th		As for 7th Jo	
"	13th		As for 7th Jo	
"	14th		As for 7th Jo	
"	15th		Coy R & F placed same Jo	

WAR DIARY

INTELLIGENCE SUMMARY.
(Erase heading not required.)

Army Form C. 2118.

December 1918   151 Field Coy R.E.

Place	Date	Hour	Summary of Events and Information	Remarks and references to Appendices
ATTICHES	16th		As for 7th	
"	17th		As for 7th	
"	18th		As for 7th	
"	19th		As for 7th	
"	20th		As for 7th	
"	21st		As for 7th	
"	22nd		Coy read lect & played games	
"	23rd		Two Off. took as for 7th. Nos 1 & 3 sections moved to Coy HQ at ATTICHES afternoon to spend Xmas with the Coy	
"	24th		Whole Coy employed preparing for Xmas festivities	
"	25th		Reg. holiday. Coy spent Xmas festivities	
"	26th		Coy Holiday, Games etc.	
"	27th		Nos 1 & 3 Sections continued work north of DA. to move back to billets at La BOVARIE. Remainder as on 7th	
"	28th		As for 7th	
"	29th		As for 7th	
"	30th		As for 7th	
"	31st		As for 7th	

Steel Major R.E.
O.C. 151 F.C. 67 R.E.
31/12/18

War Diary

of the

154th (Field) Company R.E.

From 1st January 1919 to 31st January 1919.

Army Form C. 2118.

WAR DIARY
INTELLIGENCE SUMMARY.
(Erase heading not required.)

157 FLD COY RE

JAN. 1919

Place	Date	Hour	Summary of Events and Information	Remarks and references to Appendices
ATTICHES	1st		2 Sections working with Div Artillery. One Section working on Div Workshops; One Section working on Billet works & workshops	
	2nd		As for 1st	
	3rd		As for 1st	
	4th		As for 1st	
	5th		Coy Holiday. Church parade & sports &	
	6th		As for 1st	
	7th		As for 1st	
	8th		As for 1st	
	9th		As for 1st	
	10th		As for 1st	
	11th		As for 5th	
	12th		As for 1st	
	13th		As for 1st	
	14th		As for 1st	
	15th		As for 1st. 7 men despatched for demobilization to U.K.	

Army Form C. 2118.

WAR DIARY
INTELLIGENCE SUMMARY.
(Erase heading not required.)

151 Fld Coy R.E.   JAN 1919

Place	Date	Hour	Summary of Events and Information	Remarks and references to Appendices
ATTICHES	16		As for 12th B	
	17		As for 12th B	
	18		As for 12th B	
	19		As for 8th B	
	20		As for 1st B	
	21		As for 1st O.P. ATTACHES.	
	22		No.1 Section moved from LE THEUX to CRATICHES. No. 2 & 3 Sects. worked on the 5th No.1 Section started work on erection of a heavy bridge over HAUTE DEULE Canal at COURRIERES fo. 21 Men dispatched to Ezel for demolishing fo.	
	23		No.1 Sect worked on Heavy Bridge at Courriers. Nos 2-3 & 4 Sects as for 5th B	
	24		As for 23rd B	
	25		As for 23rd B	
	26		(Sunday) Church Parade, Inspection of Games &c.	
	27		Work as for 23rd B	
	28		Work as for 23rd Aug	
	29		Work as for 23rd B 17 men sent to Ezel for Demolishing &c.	
	30		Work as for 23rd B	
	31			

O.C. 151 F.Coy R.E. [signature] 1/2/19

— CONFIDENTIAL —

War Diary
of the
157th FIELD COY R.E.

from
1st FEBRUARY 1919
31st FEBRUARY 1919

Army Form C. 2118.

WAR DIARY
INTELLIGENCE SUMMARY.
(Erase heading not required.)

FEBRUARY 1919.   157 FIELD COY RE

Place	Date	Hour	Summary of Events and Information	Remarks and references to Appendices
ATTICHES	1st		No 1 Section working on Heavy Girder Bridge over Haute Deule Canal at COURRIERES. Nos 2, 3 & 4 Sections working in workshops at ATTICHES making timber girders for above bridge.	
do	2nd		Inspection parades & Church parades. (Sunday)	
do	3rd		do for do	
do	4th		do for do	
do	5th		do for do	
do	6th		do for do	
do	7th		do for do	
do	8th		do for do	
do	9th		do for do	
do	10th		do for do	
do	11th		do for do	
do	12th		do for do	
do	13th		Away to demobilization the dismounted sections were amalgamated into one Section. Coy at CAORS strength. Work as for 1st	
do	14th		Work as for 1st	
do	15th		Work as for 1st	

WAR DIARY

INTELLIGENCE SUMMARY

Army Form C. 2118.

157 FIELD COY. R.E.

FEBRUARY 1919.

(Erase heading not required.)

Place	Date	Hour	Summary of Events and Information	Remarks and references to Appendices
ATTICHES	16th		As for 2nd Feb.	
"	17th		As for 1st "	
"	18th		" " " "	
"	19th		" " " "	
"	20th		" " 1st "	
"	21st		" " " "	
"	22nd		" " 2nd "	
"	23rd		" " 1st "	
"	24th		" " " "	
"	25th		" " 1st "	
"	26th		" " " "	
"	27th		" " 1st "	
"	28th		" " " "	

28/3/19

Steel Major R.E.
O.C. 157 FIELD COY R.E.

Army Form C. 2118.

To Lt. Col. ?
20.3.19

Vol 40

157th Field Coys.

WAR DIARY
INTELLIGENCE SUMMARY
(Erase heading not required.)

MARCH 1919

Place	Date	Hour	Summary of Events and Information	Remarks and references to Appendices
ATTICHES	1st		Work on Plate girder (timber) Bridge at Courrieres continued. Girders placed in position.	
"	2nd		(Sunday) Inspection parade & rearranging of	
"	3rd		Work on Heavy Bridge continued	
	4th		do for 3rd	
	5th		do for 3rd	
	6th		do for 3rd	
	7th		do for 3rd	
	8th		do for 3rd	
	9th		do for 3rd (Sunday)	
	10th		do for 3rd	
	11th		do for 3rd	
	12th		do for 3rd	
	13th		20 Released men transferred to 155 Fd Coys.	
			18 " " " " 156 " " "	
			13 Retained men posted from 155 Field Coy R.E.	
			13 " " " " 156 " " " "	

Army Form C. 2118.

WAR DIARY
INTELLIGENCE SUMMARY.
(Erase heading not required.)

157th FIELD COY R.E.
MARCH 1917

Place	Date	Hour	Summary of Events and Information	Remarks and references to Appendices
Attula	13th (contd)		Here transfers were made as 157 Fd. Coy R.E. was selected to be a unit of the Army of Occupation R.	
"	14th		12 Reinforcement men joined from 156 Field Coy RE	
			6 " " " " " 155 " " "	
"	15th		As for 3rd. Work on heavy bridge at Courrieres completed R.	
"	16th		R.E. Band visited 157 Coy. Officers and billets until 7.30 pm. Band gave 2 concerts, one at 3-30 pm & one at 6-30 pm R.	
"	17th		1 N.C.O. & 6 men worked on Divisional Store and loading Refs at Templeuve Sta, preparing for entraining of Cadres & Divisional Reminders. Remainder of Coy cleaning equipment etc R.	
"	18th		Work as for 17th R.	
"	19th		Coy employed on cleaning equipment etc R.	

Army Form C. 2118.

WAR DIARY
INTELLIGENCE SUMMARY.
(Erase heading not required.)

157th Field Coy R.E.

MARCH 1919

Place	Date	Hour	Summary of Events and Information	Remarks and references to Appendices
Attiches (France)	20th		As for 19th	
"	21st		As for 19th	
"	22nd		As for 19th	
"	23rd		Inspection parades, Church parades, games etc	
"	24th		As for 19th	
"	25th		As for 19th	
"	26th		As for 19th	
"	27th		As for 19th	
"	28th		Orders recd to entrain at SECLIN on 29th to proceed to Germany.	
"	29th		Coy left Attiches at 08-45 hrs, entrained at SECLIN STA. at 13-00 hrs. Left SECLIN at 16-00 hrs. 11 Lt Choyse + 11 Lt Worrall joined from 3.6" Field Coy RE. 11 Lt Brown transferred to 157" Coy RE. Nº 157 Coy RE. left 16th Div.	
DUREN (Germany)	30th		Coy continued train journey via LILLE, ATH, CHARLEROI, NAMUR + LIEGE. and arrived at DUREN (Germany) at 23-30 hrs and came under orders of C.R.E. LIGHT. DIVISION.	
BIRGEL (Germany)	31st		Coy detrained at DUREN at 10-00 hrs. and proceeded by march route to BIRGEL arriving at 13-00 hrs. Coy billeted at BIRGEL.	

1/4/19

Beeg Major RE
O.C. 157th Field Coy RE.

www.ingramcontent.com/pod-product-compliance
Lightning Source LLC
Chambersburg PA
CBHW080851230426
43662CB00013B/2075